MW00964736

For the Love of
GOD

Revealing the power, protection and hidden
treasure of the Greatest Commandment

**From library of
Orville & Shirley
Durand**

Rev. Ed and Cheryl Henderson

insight
INTERNATIONAL

For the Love of God
© 2011 by Rev. Ed and Cheryl Henderson

Published by Insight International
4739 East 91st Street, Suite 210
Tulsa, OK 74137
918-493-1718

All rights reserved. No part of this book may be reproduced or transmitted in any form or by any means, electronic or mechanical, including photocopying and recording, or by an information storage and retrieval system, without permission in writing from the author.

Unless otherwise indicated, all Scripture quotations are taken from the *King James Version* of the Bible.

The Scripture quotation marked NASB is taken from the *New American Standard Bible.* Copyright © 1960, 1962, 1963, 1968, 1971, 1972, 1973, 1975, 1977 by The Lockman Foundation. Used by permission.

All Scripture quotations marked NKJV are taken from the *New King James Version* of the Bible. Copyright © 1979, 1980, 1982, Thomas Nelson, Inc., Publishers.

The Scripture quotation marked NIV is taken from *The Holy Bible: New International Version.* Copyright © 1973, 1978, 1984 by The International Bible Society. Used by permission of Zondervan Bible Publishers.

The Scripture quotation marked NIRV is taken from *The New International Reader's Version,* Biblegateway.com. Accessed September 22, 2010.

All Scripture quotations marked AMP are taken from *The Amplified Bible, New Testament,* copyright © 1958, 1987 by The Lockman Foundation, La Habra, California; or from *The Amplified Bible, Old Testament,* copyright © 1964, 1987 by Zondervan Publishing House, Grand Rapids, Michigan.

The Scripture quotation marked NLT is taken from the *Holy Bible, New Living Translation,* copyright © 1996, 2004. Used by permission of Tyndale House Publishers, Inc., Carol Stream, Illinois 60188. All rights reserved.

The Scripture quotation marked MSG is taken from *The Message,* copyright © 1993, 1994, 1995, 1996, 2000, 2001, 2002 by Eugene H. Peterson. Used by permission of NavPress Publishing Group.

ISBN: 978-1-890900-54-0

Library of Congress catalog card number: 2010938624

Printed in the United States of America.

Dedication

This book is dedicated to all the seasoned and faithful men and women of God who have planted mighty seeds in our lives throughout our walk with the Lord.

Thank you, Pastors Fred and Valerie Bennett of Christ the Rock Church in Memphis, Tennessee, for setting a godly example for us from the beginning.

Thank you, Charlie and Carolyn Franklin, for sowing so much Word in us as our Sunday school teachers at Christ the Rock Church.

Thank you, Bishop Paul and Sharon Zink of New Life Christian Fellowship in Jacksonville, Florida, for taking us to the next level of ministry by introducing us to marketplace evangelism.

A special thank you to Brig and Lita Hart for your tremendous faithfulness to the call of God on your lives through many challenges. Because of your steadfastness, thousands are in the Kingdom of God today.

And thank you to all our partners and supporters who have faithfully supported my wife Cheryl and me and New Life (www.newlifenetwork.org) over a period of twenty-eight years. We could not do what we do without your prayers and financial support.

Most of all, we want to thank God for being exactly who He says He is in His Word, as shown to us through His Son Jesus Christ, who is the same yesterday, today and forever (Hebrews 13:8). We love You, Lord! More than yesterday, less than tomorrow!

Contents

Introduction

My wife Cheryl and I have seen and witnessed a lot over a period of twenty-eight years in the ministry of evangelism. We have had the privilege and honor of ministering in hundreds of churches and prisons and speaking to business audiences of thousands in the United States and several countries abroad.

We have counseled with hundreds of people in all types of situations. We have seen God set people free from bondages and addictions through many different types of effective ministries, such as prayer, counseling, deliverance, instantaneous miracles, laying on of hands, inner healing, twelve step programs, etc.

All of these ministry types are viable and important, but this book will deal with none of those efforts. It will outline what we have learned to be the single most powerful answer to every type of temptation, stronghold, bondage, sin or attack of the enemy. We have found over the years that God's most powerful tools are usually very simple. They are so simple that we tend to miss, discount and overlook them, thinking that the answer to our particular situation has to be more complicated and complex. God's simple but powerful answers are truly hidden treasures (Matthew 13:44).

"But I fear, lest by any means, as the serpent beguiled Eve through his subtilty, so your minds should be corrupted from the simplicity that is in Christ" (2 Corinthians 11:3).

We sincerely hope that this book will help you better know who God really is and in the process help you learn to love Him in an extravagant way. This book is *FOR the Love of God,* and hopefully it will help you distinguish between the true character and personality of God versus the character and personality of your enemy and help you be FOR GOD and not against Him. If not *For the Love of God,* we would not personally be where we are today. We share in this book our personal journey and several real life experiences with God that have caused our love of God to grow stronger and stronger over the years.

"Those things, which ye have both learned, and received, and heard, and seen in me, do: and the God of peace shall be with you" (Philippians 4:9).

This book is also a challenge and a charge to each reader, FOR THE LOVE OF GOD! Let us all wake up and understand that we are in a spiritual war and we need to know our God and His Word intimately; and we need to be careful not to place blame on Him for something the enemy has orchestrated. Your personal love of God has great rewards and is the single most powerful answer to any of your questions or problems. His sincere desire for you is for you and your family to succeed in life. God loves you, and His plans for you are for good and not for evil! (Jeremiah 29:11).

Introduction

We hope you are blessed by our story and the love of God that made it all possible.

Rev. Ed. and Cheryl Henderson

Chapter 1
The Hidden Treasure

We have heard many powerful testimonies over the years, but none so profound and moving as one we heard from a ministry friend who was a former outlaw biker. This young man was a Vietnam veteran who returned to the States, as many did, without any type of welcome home or any type of understanding from friends and family of what they had been through. The only understanding and acceptance he received was from an outlaw biker gang in California that quickly befriended him and welcomed him in as a member.

Eventually, he served as an enforcer for that gang and a bouncer for a nightclub. He would fight anybody at the drop of a hat. He sold and used drugs extensively. He was married three times, and he was responsible for seven abortions. He frequented prostitutes, robbed, stole and even beat up his own mother. His friends called him "animal" and "maniac." This was one hard, mean and degenerate individual who you did not want to meet in a dark alley or any other place.

One night, in his small California apartment, after several years of debauchery, Jesus appeared to this outlaw biker and told him that He loved him. One of the toughest and meanest guys around was shaken to the core. An all-powerful God brought this grizzly old biker to his knees that night. This was a modern-day Damascus road experience.

Our friend gave his life to Jesus Christ that night in that little apartment and everything in his life started to change after that encounter. Most of the major addictions in his life fell away immediately, but some took a little longer. (God always cleans His fish after He catches them.) Smoking cigarettes was one of the things that took a little longer to stop. This was a tough fight for him. He really wanted to quit smoking, but he couldn't seem to break that particular habit even though he had stopped using pot, cocaine and crank.

One day a pastor friend suggested that he get a blank business card and write on it, "Could I see Jesus doing this?" and place it in his shirt pocket where he kept his cigarettes. He said that became one aggravating little card! Every time he pulled his cigarettes out to take a smoke, that card would fall out of his pocket. He said he got so aggravated with it that one day he tried to throw the card away and it literally stuck to his finger. Eventually, he quit smoking because he said it did not matter how hard he tried, he could never envision in his mind Jesus smoking a cigarette.

What was the secret and power behind this particular victory? Was it his persistence? Was it the card? Was it his faith? What exactly was the secret? Do you remember what Jesus said when He was asked what was the greatest commandment? He said, *"Thou shalt love the Lord thy God with all thy heart, and with all thy soul, and with all thy mind. This is the first and great commandment"* (Matthew 22:37-38).

Our friend's victory was brought about simply by his tremendous love of God! He loved God so much that he did not want to do anything that he could not see Jesus doing. Do you remember when Jesus said He did not do anything that He did not see the Father doing and did not say anything unless He heard the Father saying it? (John 12:50). It is that type of extravagant love that breaks bondages and moves mountains. It is that type of extravagant love that creates a powerful protective shield around you and me so that the temptations of the world just fall off or bounce off. You might say it acts as a vaccination against the disease of stupid, which we are all subject to be infected by. As our love for God increases, our taste for worldly vices decreases.

This man went on to found a home for young men to help them get free of drug and alcohol addictions and come out of the lifestyle that he once walked in. Since that time he has helped thousands of men meet the God who loved him when he was so unlovable. The love of God can accomplish powerful things in a person's life and can bring hope where there appears to be no hope.

We have counseled with so many people over the years who say they love God, but at the same time they are involved in all types of terrible sins. These two things are not compatible!!! If we say we love God and are in the midst of an adulterous affair, we are liars. If we

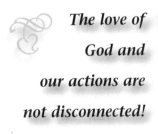

The love of God and our actions are not disconnected!

say we love God and are hooked on pornography, we are liars. We have somehow been deceived into believing that we can separate the love of God from our actions. The love of God and our actions are not disconnected! Our actions reflect to what extent we love God.

The more we truly love God, then the more we do not want to bring Him into crack houses, porn web sites, adulterous relationships and other personal areas of sin. We need to examine ourselves and our actions to see if we love God with all our heart, soul and mind, or do we just want fire insurance and at the same time still desire to be ruled by our flesh?

The following are just a few sample questions that may help you in starting this examination process:

Do you love God enough to:

1. Say "no" to your spouse or a friend?
2. Say good-bye to longtime, close friends?
3. Go to a different church than your relatives?
4. Flee fornication (including porn) and witchcraft (including drugs)?

What happens when your spouse or a friend ask you to do something or go somewhere that you know would not be pleasing to God? Do you go along anyway just to keep the peace, or do you speak up and establish a firm boundary? Are you willing to give up lifetime friendships with people who are not living for God, and are bad influences on you and your family, to have a closer relationship with God? Are you willing to walk away from the traditions of your relatives (which may or may not be good) to find out where God would have you and your family worship? Is your worship and love of God more important than your worship and love of your ancestors? Are you willing to flee pornography and drugs?

Did you know that the root Greek word used in the Bible for "fornication" is *porneia*? This is where we derive our English word "pornography" (1 Corinthians 6:18). Did you also know that the Greek word for "witchcraft" is *pharmakeia*? This is where we derive our English word "pharmacy" (Galatians 5:20).

The original sin in Genesis by Adam and Eve that got us into this mess to start with is an excellent example of how dangerous misplaced love can be. Adam had been commanded by God in Genesis 2:16-17 not to partake of the tree of the knowledge of good and evil, but in Genesis 3:6 Adam went along with Eve in partaking of this very tree. Why do you think that was? This is my personal opinion. I think Adam loved Eve so much that he was willing to do whatever she wanted just to make her happy and keep the peace. I think he loved Eve more than he loved God. He probably would not have admitted that or even thought that, but his actions shouted it. Your love for your spouse should never exceed your love for God!

I started drinking alcohol at the age of fifteen and drank pretty heavy all the way until I was thirty-five years old. My doctor had already told me that I had damaged my liver and needed to quit, but I never could quit on my own. I asked Jesus into my heart one night on a hotel room floor in

Washington, DC, after a long night of drinking. I was born again that night. My drinking decreased from that night on, but it did not completely stop until several months later.

My wife and I were in a small church in Peachtree City, Georgia, and at the end of the service the pastor asked if anyone wanted to come and pray at the altar. Cheryl and I went forward at that service and dedicated our marriage and our lives to the Lord. No one prayed for us. It was just the Lord and us.

It wasn't until several days later that I realized that the Lord had removed all my thirst for alcohol at that altar and replaced it with a thirst for His Word. That was a great day, but it did present one dilemma. All my hunting and fishing buddies drank and we had been friends for years. I actually tried to keep those friendships going, but it became very apparent that this was not going to work. I had to make a choice whether I was going to love God with all my heart and serve Him or love my friends and bow to their temptations. I chose God and I am so glad I did. I loved my friends, but I just could not hang with them.

There are some key principles here in loving God. The scriptures tell us not to have any other gods before Him (Exodus 20:3). The Word also tells us that a double-minded man will receive nothing from God and that he will be unstable in all his ways (James 1:7-8). You cannot serve God and the flesh at the same time and expect the favor, protection and blessings of God. It just does not work.

Jesus said, *"If a man love me, he will keep my words: and my Father will love him, and we will come unto him, and make our*

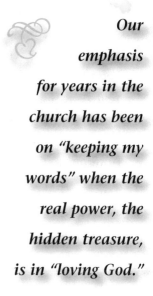

abode with him" (John 14:23). Our emphasis for years in the church has been on "keeping my words" when the real power, the hidden treasure, is in "loving God." If you really love God with all your heart, soul and mind (might) (Deuteronomy 6:5), you will not want to participate in the sins of the flesh; and keeping God's Word and His commandments will not be grievous or hard. Your heart will be protected from fear (Isaiah 35:4), your emotions will not rule you and your mind will be at peace (Isaiah 26:3).

Our emphasis for years in the church has been on "keeping my words" when the real power, the hidden treasure, is in "loving God."

"There is no fear in love; but perfect love casteth out fear: because fear hath torment. He that feareth is not made perfect in love. We love him, because he first loved us. If a man say, I love God, and hateth his brother, he is a liar: for he that loveth not his brother whom he hath seen, how can he love God whom he hath not seen? And this commandment have we from him, That he who loveth God love his brother also" (1 John 4:18-21).

"But now abide faith, hope, love, these three; but the greatest of these is love" (1 Corinthians 13:13 NASB).

The remainder of this book is dedicated to trying to help you know who God is and to help you love Him extravagantly. It is hard to love someone that you do not know intimately. It is important to know how they feel about you, what their intentions are toward you, what their dreams and visions are for you and whether you can trust them or not. No one can make you fall in love with someone. You have to spend time with that person and hopefully the time you spend in this book and the Book (the Bible), will help you realize just how much God loves you. The truth will help you love God more and more, for it is that type of extravagant love that has the power to set you free from all bondages and protect you from all enemies.

Chapter 2

The Nature of God

It is so amazing to me the different ways people think about God. Some people think of God as a mean old bearded man sitting in Heaven just waiting to hit us over the head with a big stick the first time we mess up. Some people, based on their beliefs, think that God is a murderer who takes the lives of their children and family (even though they would never admit it). Others think that God represents just a list of rules and regulations.

Recently, Cheryl and I were at a large Christian leaders' meeting where hundreds of the top evangelical leaders in the United States were in attendance. At the opening ceremony, the head of this organization and a well-known Christian author spent thirty to forty-five minutes talking about where we are as Christians in today's economic world. They acknowledged that a lot of people were suffering personally and financially in their businesses and families due to present economic conditions and that God was trying to teach us lessons through these sufferings.

No mention was ever made of our enemy (Satan) who is the instigator of all this heartache. Yes, God can teach us through sufferings, but He does not orchestrate the sufferings. We have to realize that we have an enemy, and it is time for Christians to get violent and mad at the real enemy. When we leave Satan out of the conversation, we by default (even if it is unintentional), shift the blame toward God, which negatively affects our trust of God and our love for God.

How we perceive God is very important in determining how much we love God, how strong our faith is and what we can ask and expect from God. Let me tell you a personal story that illustrates this point.

When I was about ten years of age, my parents were faithful members of a denominational church in South Georgia. I attended Sunday school every Sunday, and my relationship with Jesus was growing. I can remember dedicating my life to Jesus and feeling very close to the Lord. Then one Sunday my family and I went to visit my grandparents, who lived on a small farm about sixty miles away. My grandfather was very religious and loved to sing in his country church choir, and he always attended the local Southern gospel quartet sings that were very popular at that time in rural Georgia.

When we arrived at my grandparents' home in South Georgia, which was out in the country on several acres, I immediately noticed that their yard was all grown up and in need of mowing. That was very unusual because their property was usually immaculate. My grandfather was gone when we first arrived and my grandmother told my mother that he had been ill and could not keep up with the yard work. He was getting up in years by this time, in his seventies. So I thought this would be a great time to be a good Samaritan and get his old lawn mower out and cut the grass for him, and that is what I proceeded to do.

My grandfather returned home about the time I was half through with the yard, and rather than being happy for my help, he was furious. He made me stop cutting the yard, turn the lawn mower off, and looked at me with this mean and disgusted look. He said, "Boy, have you lost your religion? Don't you know that you are not supposed to work on Sunday?"

That incident was devastating to a ten year old who was just trying to help his grandfather. I remember thinking that I did not want to serve a God who would not even let you help someone on Sundays.

I was thirty-five years old before I ever went back to serving God. It wasn't until I began to read the Bible that I learned that my grandfather did not really know God in an intimate way. He had religion, but religion can be very hard. Second Corinthians 3:6 tells us that the letter of the law kills, but the Spirit gives life. Mark 7:13 tells us that the traditions of men make the Word of God of no effect.

It is so important for all of us, and especially children, to know the true nature of God and not just what man

It is so important for all of us, and especially children, to know the true nature of God and not just what man thinks.

21

thinks. God's nature in this particular case is embodied in the scriptures where Jesus plucked ears of corn to feed His disciples on the Sabbath and healed a man with a withered hand on the Sabbath (Mark 2:23-3:6). The Pharisees (religious leaders of that day) did not like these actions at all and initiated their plans to destroy Jesus because He would not line up with their traditions.

So thinking back on it now, my heart was right as a child, but the sad part about it was that years of service were stolen because I did not really know and understand the true nature of God, which is displayed for all of us in the Bible through the life of Jesus. *"He that hath seen me hath seen the Father . . ."* (John 14:9).

The heart of God is reflected throughout the scriptures as compassionate and loving, with a deep desire for His kids to prosper, succeed and win. The Lord said, *"For I know the thoughts that I think toward you, saith the Lord, thoughts of peace* [not calamity], *and not for evil* [but good], *to give you an expected end* [hope]" (Jeremiah 29:11).

In Hebrews 12:1 it mentions a great cloud of witnesses. I have always looked at that as God, the angels and the saints who have gone before us, looking over the banisters of Heaven and rooting for you and me. Why is all this so important? *"As a man thinketh in his heart, so is he . . ."* (Proverbs 23:7). If you and I think that God is against us, are we encouraged or discouraged? The knowledge that God is for us, rooting for us to succeed, prosper and win is very encouraging. It helps us through the tough times and helps us beat back all the confusion, lies and doubts that Satan, the world and religion can throw at us.

You have to personally know God's heart for yourself. Be encouraged! God is for you! He wants you to succeed, regardless of where you have been in the past. He wants you to win.

Cheryl's Insights

Early in our marriage we were living in Jonesboro, Georgia, just outside of Atlanta. Ed was working as a Federal Investigator, and I was having a great time selling real estate and modeling. We had one son at the time and he was eight years old. I was near my family for the first time in several years, and I was enjoying the family get-togethers I had missed while we lived in faraway places. In other words, I was happy doing MY thing.

I went to the doctor for a checkup, and he delivered news that sent me into a tizzy!!! He informed me that I was pregnant!! "I beg your pardon . . . you must be mistaken" was my first response. He assured me that he knew what he was talking about. Well, needless to say, another baby was not in my plans. I mean, how in the world do you model when you are fat? This was the 70's and thin was in!!

I threw a hissie fit in that office! The doctor took me by the shoulders, looked me straight in the eyes, and said. "Young lady, the Lord has His hands in this!" I jerked away and responded, "Well, the Lord doesn't have to get up for the two o'clock feeding!" I can't believe I acted like that, but I was just living for myself and my selfish, carnal nature was in control.

When I arrived home that day with the news, Ed informed me that we had been transferred to Miami, Florida. To add insult to injury, Ed was elated that I was pregnant and that made me even madder! In one afternoon my whole world was turned upside down. Not only was I going to have a baby, but also we were being uprooted from everything I loved about my life at that time. I just sat down in the kitchen floor and began to cry.

Ed looked down at me and said, "What's wrong with you?" I said, "First, I want a divorce, then I want an abortion and then I am going to kill myself!" Ed very calmly said, "Well, if you are going to do the last one, why worry about the first two?" Were we crazy or what? The fact of the matter was, I was NOT going to kill myself. (I don't like pain and I loved me too much for that.) I was not going to have an abortion. Even in my selfish and lost state, I knew that was murder, and what woman divorces her husband when she is pregnant and needs him to take care of her and pay the bills?

So, we moved to the Miami, Florida, area and I prepared myself to have another baby. The little house we purchased in Sunrise, Florida, needed a lot of work. We jumped right in and began painting and getting it ready for us to live in. By this time I was about seven months along.

One morning I woke up to the bed being soaking wet. I had no clue what was going on. By that afternoon, I discovered that my water had broke. I went to the doctor and he put me right in the hospital. By that evening, Donald (Chip) Henderson was born. Ed had been at the hospital all day with our other son David and they were very tired. As soon as the baby was born, and things seemed okay, they left for home. However, I woke up in the recovery room with someone waving a piece of paper in my face, saying, "Sign this, sign this. Your baby is not breathing well, and we are not sure what is going on. We have to do a spinal tap. Sign this." This was before the days of cell phones and Ed was between the hospital and home. I somehow scribbled my name on the paper.

In the 70's, women were given a medication called twilight. You were sort of asleep and you could assist in the delivery, but you would not remember it. When I was coherent enough to walk down to the nursery, I saw that precious, tiny, perfect baby in an incubator with tubes in everything you could put a tube into. My heart sank and I was overcome with guilt. This was the baby I didn't want. How could I be so selfish? He didn't ask for this. I looked at that tiny chest pumping up and down as hard as it could go, gasping for every breath. I felt horrible.

About that time, the doctor walked up and said, "Mrs. Henderson, we are doing all we can do. I just don't know if this baby will live or die." At that moment, the words of my doctor in Atlanta came flooding back to me and I turned to the doctor and responded with a faith I did not know I had. "Well I know! God has His hands in this and He deals with everlasting life, not death. This baby will live and not die!" The words of my doctor in Atlanta were so important to me. They were life to me, and God brought them to my remembrance when I needed them.

I can't begin to tell you how my faith in God and my love grew for God after that situation. He loved me even when I was unlovable. That baby stands 6'7" today and is a fine man of God with a beautiful wife and two fine sons of his own. We serve a mighty God!

"He sent his word, and healed them, and delivered them from their destructions" (Psalm 107:20).

"Who forgiveth all thine iniquities; who healeth all thy diseases . . ." (Psalm 103:3).

"Beloved, I wish above all things that thou mayest prosper and be in health, even as thy soul prospereth" (3 John 2).

Chapter 3

God Unjustly Accused

The national and local news reports were replete with the untimely deaths of major entertainment and television personalities, such as singer and "King of Pop" Michael Jackson; actress and "Charlie's Angel" Farrah Fawcett; infomercial king Billy Mays; and retired NFL Super Bowl quarterback Steve McNair. It is never easy to lose a loved one, and we grieved with and prayed for all the family members in each of these situations.

As awful and tragic as each of these cases were, we need to understand and learn several critical spiritual lessons through these types of events. Number one, life is very precious and very fragile. Number two, the Bible tells us that death is an enemy and that it is the thief (Satan) who comes to kill, steal and destroy, not God (John 10:10). Jesus came to give us life and life more abundantly, not death.

> *Untimely death is not God's way of filling vacant positions in Heaven.*

Untimely death is not God's way of filling vacant positions in Heaven.

I get so upset when I hear people at funerals and memorial services attribute an untimely death to God. If this is God's doing, then we need to stop praying for the sick, close all our hospitals and quit fighting sickness, disease, addictions, injuries and death, because we would be fighting against God. The God that I know is crying and brokenhearted over each and every untimely death.

Worldly and religious thinking and language foster this pattern of unjustly accusing God for every disaster and every death, which can severely influence a person's love of God. Our insurance companies describe such things as hurricanes and earthquakes as "acts of God." The definition of "acts of God" in www.answers.com is "a manifestation, especially of a violent or destructive natural force, such as a lightning strike or an earthquake, that is beyond human power to cause, prevent or control."

Have you ever been unjustly accused of some crime or misdeed? How did it make you feel? How do you think God feels? Is it any wonder that people don't want to serve God? They think that any moment He is going to strike them dead or put cancer on their children. Who would want to serve a God or love a God like that?

Even people in the Bible had this same misconception about God. A prime example was the story of Job. There is a famous quote that was made by Job that is repeated over and over again by preachers and theologians that depicts God as a murderer and depicts Job as a great man of faith. Job said,

"Though he slay me, yet will I trust in him" (Job 13:15). Job obviously thought God was trying to slay him, but it is evident in Job 1:7-12 that it was Satan who was the culprit in this incident. And then some preachers and theologians take this situation one step further and teach that nothing can happen to a Christian without it first coming across the desk of God. This means that God approves all the attacks of the enemy, including sickness, disease, disasters, murder, etc. Hogwash!!!

The God that I know and worship is not a mafia boss! He is God, and He is Father, but He is not a Godfather. In my opinion, Job was a one-time example that God used to roll back the spiritual curtain to give us a glimpse of the spiritual battle that is constantly being waged and the protection that He places around His kids.

The God that I know and worship is not a mafia boss!

> *"And the Lord said unto Satan, Hast thou considered my servant Job, that there is none like him in the earth, a perfect and an upright man, one that feareth God, and escheweth evil? Then Satan answered the Lord, and said, Doth Job fear God for nought? Hast not thou made an hedge about him, and about his house, and about all that he hath on every side? Thou hast blessed the work of his hands, and his substance is increased in the land."* (Job 1:8-10).

We need to go back to Genesis (the beginning) and understand where death and sickness came from. God's creation contained eternal life with no sickness and no death. Death and sickness entered in by the sin of Adam and Eve. God told them if they partook of the tree of the knowledge of good and evil they would surely die.

Let me ask you this question. Is there death in Heaven? Is their sickness in Heaven? NO, NO, NO, and emphatically NO!!! *"And God shall wipe away all tears from their eyes; and there shall be no more death, neither sorrow, nor crying, neither shall there be any more pain: for the former things are passed away"* (Revelation 21:4).

Let me ask you a second set of questions. Did you ever see Jesus sick? How did He react to sickness? *"He healed them all"* (Matthew 12:15)!!! How did Jesus react to storms? He rebuked the storm (Mark 4:35-41)!!! Now either Jesus was being disobedient to God or He was God, showing us what He thought about sickness and storms. I choose the latter.

We all need to wake up and realize we are in a spiritual war!! You and I have an enemy and his name is Satan, the devil. He is a stealth bomber, and his very nature is to lie and deceive. He is invisible and his attacks are made when you least suspect them. His ultimate goal is to kill, steal and destroy (John 10:10), and then blame it all on God. What a sweet deal!

His weapons are old, but they are still very potent. They include such things as alcohol, sex, drugs, adultery, sickness, disease, unforgiveness, greed, pride, hate, etc. All of these fall under the simple category of sin, and usually they are wrapped in a very pretty package, but the end result is the same. *"The wages of sin is death . . ."* (Romans 6:23), but thank God, we have been given a way of escape and we have been given armor and weapons that are mighty through God to fight these battles and pull down these strongholds.

If you have accepted Jesus Christ as your Savior, then you have the Holy Spirit residing inside of you and the Holy Spirit, in conjunction with the Word of God, will be your guide and protector. God has provided certain fences that we are all to live within and they are for our protection.

A faithful marriage is an example of one such fence that protects us from all types of sexually transmitted diseases that could lead to death. Abstaining from the use of drugs and alcohol is another fence that God has placed for our protection. Most all of these types of sins will start very innocently, but they have a tendency to always escalate. *"Hell and destruction are never full; so the eyes of man are never satisfied."* (Proverbs 27:20). The ultimate goal of the enemy is always death, whether that be physical death, death of a relationship, death of a business, death of your finances, death of a marriage or any other type of death.

I had an old preacher tell me one time, "If you let the devil in the car with you, he will eventually want to drive." That is the simplest way I know to look at some of these situations. The devil is a hitchhiker. If you have accepted Jesus Christ, then the devil has no power over you unless you invite him into your car. If you let him in the car and you let him drive, eventually you will end up in a ditch somewhere.

I heard a song one time that talked about enjoying the fences that God has put us in. In this smorgasbord-of-sin atmosphere that we are all surrounded by, we need to abide within and enjoy those fences. God's fences are not there to keep you and me from experiencing life. They are there to keep you and me from experiencing untimely death due to our own choices.

> *"As righteousness tendeth to life: so he that pursueth evil pursueth it to his own death"* (Proverbs 11:19).

> *"For the wages of sin is death; but the gift of God is eternal life through Jesus Christ our Lord"* (Romans 6:23).

> *"I call heaven and earth to record this day against you, that I have set before you life and death, blessing and cursing: therefore choose life, that both thou and thy seed may live"* (Deuteronomy 30:19).

We encourage you to choose life today!!! We are convinced that God's desire is for each of us to live a long and prosperous life.

Chapter 4

Learning to Love God

At this point you may be asking the question, "How do I learn to love God more?" That is a very good question, and we will try to give you some pointers, suggestions and share some personal experiences in this chapter and the chapters that follow which will hopefully help.

Have you ever been in love? I mean, head over heels in love with someone! If so, how did that happen? In most cases, it was a process of meeting someone and then getting to know them over a period of time. It is impossible to really love someone you don't even know! Have you ever had a brief encounter with someone that you thought you could really love and then after you spent some time with them, you learned that you did not even like that individual?

On the other hand, have you ever met someone and immediately wrote them off as someone you would never like and then later, after spending time with them, you learned that they had a great personality and they became a lifelong friend and trusted companion?

Learning to love God can be very similar to that. We all have preconceived ideas of who God is and how He reacts to us. Most of these perceptions come from religion, family members or friends, and most of them are usually nowhere near the truth. That is why you need to have a personal encounter and a personal relationship with God. You need to know the truth for yourself, and that takes an effort on your part to spend time with Him.

My wife Cheryl committed her life to the Lord four years before I did. I was very distrustful of preachers and religious individuals, but I knew my wife very well and some things were changing in her life that I could not deny. As a result of my wife's changing lifestyle and changing heart, I started secretly reading the Bible. At first, I was reading it for all the wrong reasons. I mainly wanted to somehow justify my lifestyle by scripture (which many of us do), so I was always quick to point out certain scriptures like "a little wine is good for the stomach." But to find those type of scriptures, I had to read a lot of other stuff that started me on a path to knowing and loving God.

I read through the entire Bible at least twice before I committed my life to the Lord. I wanted to assure myself that this God and this Jesus talked about in the Bible were real and that this was not just some emotional, religious sales job perpetrated by fancy talking preachers.

We believe the following steps will help you to know God. If you really know God, then we know that you will really love Him.

Read the Bible

The first suggestion we would give to anyone wanting to know and love God would be to read His Word (the Bible). The Bible is the heartbeat of God. It contains His words that are settled in Heaven forever and ever (Psalm 119:89). It contains His commandments that are there for your protection. It contains His promises that are there for you and me to claim by faith. It contains His wisdom and instructions for your life that will help you walk through this crazy world that we all live in, and it contains the answers to all your questions, from life to death.

We don't have a lot of leisure time to go to the movies anymore, but Cheryl and I went to the movies recently to see "The Book of Eli" with Denzel Washington. If you can get past the extreme violence and some bad language, this movie does have some very profound lessons related to the Book (the Bible).

I will try my best not to ruin the movie for anyone who hasn't seen it yet. The plot is described by www.imdb.com as follows. Eli (Denzel Washington) has been on a journey for thirty years, walking west across America after a cataclysmic war that turned the earth into a total wasteland. The world has become a lawless civilization where people must kill or be killed. The barren roads belong to gangs of cutthroats who rob and kill for water, a pair of shoes, a lighter or just for fun.

Eli is a peaceful man who only acts in self-defense, and becomes a warrior with unbelievable killing skills when he is challenged. After the war and the "Big Flash," Eli was guided by a higher power to a hidden book and given the task of protecting the book and taking it to its final destination. Eli guards the book with his life, because he knows that <u>the book is the only hope that humanity has for its future</u>.

There is a constant battle in the movie between good and evil over the <u>possession</u> of the Book (the Bible). Some will kill to have it. He (Eli) will kill to protect it. There is a very powerful truth that comes to light at the very end of this movie and that truth is this:

THE POWER IS NOT IN THE MAN WITH THE BOOK, BUT IN THE BOOK IN THE MAN. (You will probably need to see the movie to totally understand.)

The first chapter of the Gospel of John tells us, *"In the beginning was the Word, and the Word was with God, and the Word was God . . . And the Word was made flesh, and dwelt among us . . ."* (vv. 1, 14). These scriptures are talking about Jesus. He was the Word and He became flesh and dwelt among us. You and I are just the opposite.

We are flesh that needs to be made the Word.

We are flesh that needs to be made the Word. The Word has no power if it is just sitting on our coffee table or on a bookshelf. It has to become part of us. James 1:21 describes it as an "engrafted" Word. You and I need a skin graft of the Word kind, and the only way to get that accomplished is to spend time in the Word. The Word is quick, powerful and sharper than any two-edged sword. It will bring power into your life. It will fight your battles for you. It will give you direction. It will protect you and bring peace in difficult times.

I remember a time when I was in Dallas, Texas, working for several weeks, and I received a frantic phone call from my wife in Memphis. Our youngest son had been climbing in a neighbor's tree and had fallen out of the tree on his right arm. Cheryl had taken him to the emergency room and the doctor had put the arm in a cast and told my wife he thought my son had broken the growth plate in his arm.

Here come those negative thoughts flooding in: "My son's arm will be deformed. He will not be able to pitch a ball or play sports." I knew God well enough by now to recognize where all those thoughts came from and they weren't from God. I told Cheryl to let me pray and I would call her back, so I started to walk around my motel room and pray.

As I prayed and worshipped God, a scripture that I had memorized came back to me from Proverbs 4:20-22, which says: *"My son, attend to my words; incline thine ear unto my sayings. Let them not depart from thine eyes; keep them in the midst of thine heart. For they are life unto those that find them, and health to all their flesh."* As I quoted that scripture from memory, I heard God say, "Your son Chip is your flesh." I knew immediately that was God because I had always interpreted that verse selfishly to mean that "all their flesh" meant my flesh.

I immediately picked up the phone and called Cheryl and told her what God had said and told her not to worry, that Chip was going to be fine. Chip went on to be a pitcher and also receive a basketball scholarship to college. What do you think that did for our faith and for our love of God?

We encourage you today to spend time with the Book (the Bible). Let it become so familiar to you that it is a compass for you and leads you just like it led Eli in the movie. When trials come, we run to the Word and not to the world. Let it become your sword of the Spirit that you can use to do battle against all enemies. Let it become your personal prophet that will guide your actions and shield you from harm. Let it be your salvation, your deliverance and your healer.

When trials come, we run to the Word and not to the world.

The Word can do all those things and more, for it is truly the only hope that humanity has for its future.

Get Born Again

The second suggestion we would give to anyone wanting to know and love God would be to get born again (Romans 10:9). The scriptures tell us that we cannot even see the Kingdom of God unless we are born again (John 3:3). God gives all of us enough faith and enough understanding to make a choice between life and death. He wants us to choose life, but it is still our choice. If you choose life and are born again, the Holy Spirit comes to reside in you and He is the One who will lead, guide and teach you.

You will now have an understanding of the scriptures available to you that you did not have before. It was the Holy Spirit who inspired men to write the Word of God, and it is therefore the Holy Spirit who can best teach you the scriptures if you are faithful to read, study and meditate on them.

See our article on "Salvation" at www.newlifenetwork.org for more specific information on getting "Born Again."

Go to Church

The third suggestion we would give to anyone wanting to know and love God would be to find a good local church to be a part of. One of New Life Network's main focuses over the last twenty-eight years of ministry has been to help people find the "RIGHT" church. We are big believers in participation in a local church congregation, and we have assisted literally thousands of people find good church homes. As with anything else, over time you begin to recognize red flags and begin to develop some criteria on what to look for and what to be wary of.

See our article on "Choosing the Right Church" at www.newlifenetwork.org for more specific information on this subject.

Get Baptized in Water

The fourth suggestion we would give to anyone wanting to know and love God would be to get baptized in water after being born again.

I am reminded of a very important time in my life when I was baptized in water. I had recently given my life to the

Lord in Washington, DC, and was traveling on a work assignment in Houston, Texas. I was there on a Wednesday night, so I went to visit the original Lakewood Church where John Osteen, father of Joel Osteen, was the pastor. He preached on water baptism that summer night.

My religious upbringing included being baptized as a child with the sprinkling method. That night Pastor Osteen went through all the scriptures about the importance of water baptism (immersion in water) after giving your life to the Lord. I was touched that night and knew that I needed to do this.

Pastor Osteen asked everyone who had been moved by his message to stand and make a commitment to the Lord that the next time we had an opportunity, we would get baptized in water. I stood that night and made that promise to the Lord.

Many months later, my wife and I had started sharing our testimony and preaching in local churches in the Memphis, Tennessee, area. One very cold Sunday morning, we were to speak at a local Memphis congregation; and as we were preparing to speak, the pastor told me that they needed to take care of one last bit of business before we spoke. The pastor told us a young man had given his life to the Lord that week, and they were going to baptize him before we spoke.

They did not have a baptismal tank, so they had purchased a kiddie pool and filled it up with cold water. (It was about 20 degrees that winter morning.) This kiddie pool was the type that had pictures of animals all around the sides. God does have a sense of humor!

I knew what I had to do that morning. I asked a very surprised pastor if he would mind if his speaker could be baptized along with the new convert. He agreed and that is where I was baptized. It was a wonderful, but very cold baptism.

We believe that baptism in water is a very important step in your walk with the Lord. It is not, as some religions teach, mandatory for your salvation. It is, however, an outward expression to the world and to yourself of what has already transpired inwardly. If you are doing it just because some religion says you must do it, then forget it. There is no magic in the water or in the process. But if you are doing it because you love the Lord and want to follow His example, you want to sincerely please Him, and you understand from the Word of God why you are doing it, then you need to be baptized. God always looks on the heart and not on rituals, ceremonies or outward appearances (1 Samuel 16:7).

See our article on "Baptized In Water" at www.newlifenetwork.org for more specific information on this subject.

Get Baptized in the Spirit

The fifth suggestion we would give to anyone wanting to know and love God would be to get baptized in the Spirit. One of the events that helped my wife and me to love God the most was when we were baptized in the Spirit. This is a miraculous event that is a subsequent event to your salvation and is a promise to you from God (Acts 2:39).

See our article entitled "Your Appointment with Power" at www.newlifenetwork.org for more specific information on this miraculous promise.

Do the Word

The sixth suggestion we would give to anyone wanting to know and love God would be to do the Word. It is not enough to merely hear the Word. You must be a doer of the Word before you really come to know and love God and completely understand His Word (James 1:22-25).

CAUTION!! There are three times in your life when you will probably change friends. The first is when you get born again. The second is when you get baptized in the Spirit. The third is when you start doing what God has called you to do.

Chapter 5

Being Led By the Love of God

Some people believe that all our steps are ordered by God or by some mysterious fate, and therefore we have no say in our own destiny. Some people believe in predestination down to the point that anything that happens (good or bad) is somehow planned or approved by God. Let's take a close look at the scriptures to determine what is the truth.

Psalm 37:23 says, *"The steps of a good man [or woman] are ordered by the Lord. . . ."* That would appear to some to prove that God is in charge of our every step. Let's look at it a little closer. The word "ordered" is the key here. The Hebrew word used in this context is *kuwn*, which means prepared, provided, established,

God has definitely prepared a way for us to walk in that is right and prosperous, but it is still up to us to seek it out and walk in it.

ordained, right, proper and prosperous. God has definitely prepared a way for us to walk in that is right and prosperous, but it is still up to us to seek it out and walk in it.

Let me ask you this question. Why would God instruct us to go into all the world and preach the gospel if everyone's destiny had already been determined? God made us all free moral agents. He did not make us robots.

The first step you must take is to be equipped with the sight to see the way. Jesus said in John 14:6, *"I am the way, the truth, and the life: no man cometh unto the Father, but by me."* Notice, He did not say He was one of the ways but THE WAY. Jesus also said in John 3:3, *"Except a man be born again, he cannot see the kingdom of God."* So the first step is to be born again so you can see the right path.

Looking back on the steps Cheryl and I have taken since dedicating our lives to the Lord, we can clearly see major turning points in our journey. One such turning point was when I ministered in a county jail in Mississippi. I had a friend in Memphis who went into jails and prisons on a regular basis, and he asked me one day if I wanted to go. I said, "Sure," not knowing what to expect.

When we arrived at this particular county jail in North Mississippi, they immediately searched us and took us behind a big steel door that slammed and locked behind us. In my mind, I thought we were probably going to be both led to a chapel so we could preach to the men while the guards protected us. So much for vain imaginations!

What they did was separate us and put us in separate bull pens. The bull pen consisted of one big room with bunk beds stacked around each wall, three bunks high. Each bull pen had about twenty to thirty inmates. The jailer escorted me into this bull pen and said, "Have at it," and locked me in the room with twenty to thirty inmates and turned around and left.

This is where you get to find out if you really know God or are you just playing a religious game. Prisoners can recognize a phony in about two seconds. I am happy to tell you that I survived and the men were ministered to. It might not have been eloquent, but it was real.

When I left that county jail that day, something happened to me that is very hard to explain. When I walked outside and looked into the sky, I literally felt God smile. This is one of those things that you have to experience to understand, because I never recall reading anything in my *King James Bible* about God smiling, but the following scripture took on new meaning after that experience: *"For the joy of the Lord is your strength"* (Nehemiah 8:10).

This is one of those scriptures that we usually read very selfishly and thus miss a much deeper meaning. Usually we interpret this scripture to mean that we are the ones who are joyous and not the Lord. Believe me, when God smiles, His joy will bring you strength. This is why it is so important to do the Word, because when you do the Word, the scriptures come alive and take on unselfish meanings we would have never thought about. Also, they will change how you relate to God.

> *Believe me, when God smiles, His joy will bring you strength.*

"Thou wilt shew me the path of life: in thy presence is full-ness of joy; at thy right hand there are pleasures for ever-more" (Psalm 16:11). (Unselfish = God is full of joy!!!)

"May the Lord smile on you and be gracious to you" (Numbers 6:25 NLT).

"Let your face smile on me with favor. Teach me your orders" (Psalm 119:135 NIRV).

"Warm me, your servant, with a smile: save me because you love me" (Psalm 31:16 MSG).

After that first visit, Cheryl and I went on to minister in hundreds of jails and prisons in several different states. God taught us so much while we ministered to the men and women who are incarcerated.

Another major turning point was when I was offered a promotion and would need to move from Memphis, Tennessee, to Jacksonville, Florida. In our mind, we thought we would retire in the Memphis area. We did not know for sure if this was the right step, so I took off work for several days and went to a cabin in the woods to read the Word and pray.

One of the scriptures that I read during that time was in the book of Hebrews. It was about Abraham and how he was called to go out into a new and unfamiliar place and in that place he would receive an inheritance (blessing) and he obeyed. It was that time with God and His Word that confirmed the next step to take. The step was there, it was prepared, but I had to seek God to confirm it and ultimately make the choice to step out.

About one year after moving to Jacksonville, Florida, Cheryl and I met Brig and Lita Hart and were asked to start New Life Network. We have seen thousands of people come into the Kingdom of God since that time, but that would have never happened in our lives if we had not taken that first step. There have also been many attempts by the enemy along the way to knock us off that path, and he will do the same to you. That is his job. Your job is to stay faithful to your calling, regardless of what anyone says or does.

Cheryl's Insights

I grew up in a loving, fun, but somewhat dysfunctional family. We had lots of fun in our home, because my three brothers were all musicians and played in local nightclubs and other venues all around Atlanta, Georgia. One of my brothers went on to be a country western entertainer, and in the 70's and 80's, he had over forty chart records to his credit. Often, he was on the Grand Ole Opry. He is now in the Georgia Music Hall of Fame. Music and get-togethers were an every Sunday affair. Mama's fried chicken dinners and a family jam session was the norm for Sunday afternoons.

The dysfunction came into the household due to my father's drinking problem. He was more of a binge drinker. He would stay sober for weeks and even months, and then all of a sudden he would go on a drinking binge. He was never violent or abusive, but his drinking caused havoc in our family routine, brought on financial strife, and I know my mother suffered the most dealing with an alcoholic.

Despite all of that, I was very close to my dad. He was always such an encourager to me. He often told me I could do anything. He always told me I was beautiful. He was always telling me how much he loved me. So when I started getting into God's Word and committed my life to the Lord, it was easy for me to receive the Lord as Abba (Daddy) God. He just reminded me of my earthly father.

Now I realize that not everyone has had a great experience with his or her earthly father. I know that many have never even known their fathers. I also realize that bad relationships with parents can affect how we might perceive God the Father. If this describes you, I recommend that you imagine the most perfect, wonderful, supportive, encouraging and loving father, multiply that by a thousand, and then you will come a little closer to your heavenly Father. He truly is so good there is no way to describe it, and He loves you beyond anything you can imagine.

Ed and I and the boys were visiting my parents in Atlanta one summer while on vacation. By this time, my dad was not only in his seventies, but he had given his life to Jesus and was delivered from alcohol. My mother's prayers were answered, and they were in the happiest time of their lives.

Dad had been taking a leadership training course at his church. He wanted to be a better public speaker and to have more confidence in getting up in front of people. His graduation was that weekend, and he had to give his final speech. He had asked Ed for some help on finding several scriptures he wanted to use in his speech. I never thought I would see the day that my father and my husband would be reading the Word together!!

God is truly amazing in how He does things exceedingly, abundantly more than we can ask or think. One of the scriptures was from Psalm 90:10 that promises us threescore and ten years, and then we will fly away. My dad loved that old song, "I'll Fly Away."

The next morning Ed and I and the boys left Atlanta and went to Albany, Georgia, to see his parents for a few days. On the second day we were there, I received a phone call from my brother telling me that my father had experienced a massive heart attack and he was now in Heaven. He told me that Dad went to his graduation and got up and gave his speech. At the end of his speech, he said to his audience that it really didn't matter whether he became a great speaker or not. He had already been given his threescore and ten years, but what really mattered was his faith in God, because in the end we will all fly away. He went back to his seat, his head went over on the table, and he went home to be with Jesus right there! What a testimony!!

Now you have to know that I was heartsick over losing my dad. It was so sudden. I didn't have time to prepare myself. I knew where he was and that gave me great comfort, but I missed him!!! I missed his phone calls, I missed his encouragement, I missed his laughter and I missed him!! I really experienced some serious grief.

After the funeral, we went back to our home in Tennessee. Things went back to normal. Ed went to work, the kids went to school and I went back to my daily routine as a housewife. One day, while I was hanging my sheets on the clothesline outside, I noticed how beautiful the sky was. What a glorious day it was, but I still missed my dad horribly. My heart was so heavy and it hurt down deep. As I was going through the process of putting the sheets on the line, I heard an audible voice say, "I'm your Daddy now!" I hit my knees in the grass and sobbed! I was there for quite some time, crying so loud that I thought the neighbors would call 911.

After I could not cry anymore, I got up and went back to hanging out my sheets. As I did, I noticed that all the grief and the heavy heart were gone! It's like God just took it away! God revealed a new part of His character to me that day. I had always known Him as God the Father, but now I knew Him as Daddy God! My love for Him increased in such a way I cannot explain. His love for me was revealed in how He wanted to comfort me and let me know things would be okay.

The next nine chapters of this book are dedicated to helping you to be led by the love of God and helping you know Him and love Him more intimately. It is not enough to just believe in God. The devils believe (James 2:19). As you spend time with God and His Word, you will develop the ability to recognize His voice just like you recognize your closest loved one's voice. As you do the Word, your faith will be built up as you see God do what He promises He will do and He will give you direction and answers for your life. A theory about God can always be stolen, but an experience with God can never be stolen.

A theory about God can always be stolen, but an experience with God can never be stolen.

Chapter 6

You Have More Authority Than You Think

As a former federal law enforcement officer, I had certain authority given to me to investigate and make arrests for certain federal crimes. As an employee of most businesses and corporations, you are given certain authority, which is usually defined by a job description. As a parent, you have certain authority concerning your children. We have all been given some type of worldly authority and for the most part we pretty well understand that authority. But most of the people we counsel with have very little understanding of the authority they have been given by God, which is the most powerful authority of all. When you understand the authority that has been given to the believer, you will love and trust God even more.

In Genesis 1:28 God gave man dominion (authority) and told man (male and female) to subdue the earth. In Luke 10:19 Jesus gave His disciples authority over Satan and all his cohorts. Acts 1:8 describes the awesome power (authority) that is given to those who receive the Holy Spirit. Ephesians 6:10-18 describes the armor of God (offensive and defensive) that has been provided to the believer. So why do we have so many people, and especially Christians, who seem to be so powerless and without any authority to overcome life's battles?

The quick and simple answer is that most people believe that God has already approved or initiated the challenge or they have been deceived into believing that their problem is their wife, their husband, their boss, their mother-in-law, the government, politicians, etc. Their battle is always with flesh and blood, which is the very reason they are losing the fight. Ephesians 6:12 states, *"For we wrestle not against flesh and blood, but against principalities, against powers, against the rulers of darkness of this world, against spiritual wickedness in high places."*

Some people spend their entire life battling the things they can see when they should be battling the things that they cannot see.

Some people spend their entire life battling the things they can see when they should be battling the things that they cannot see. The things that you see are temporal. The things that you do not see are eternal. In actuality, the things that are invisible are more real than the things that are visible, because the visible things are passing away. You do have an enemy and his name is Satan. He is the father of lies, and the person he lies to the most is you.

He knows that you have authority over him if Jesus Christ is living inside you, so what does he do? He convinces you and me that a flesh and blood human or a worldly circumstance is the problem, and he will cause you to waste all your energy and attention on that person or circumstance rather than taking authority over the spirits that are trying to steal your marriage, your children, your money and your peace. He may even convince you that it is all God's fault and it is hopeless to fight against God.

Have you ever dealt with the lies and manipulations of a crack addict? That is the nature of Satan.

Wake up!!! You are in a spiritual war and your weapons are not carnal and they are not being used! You cannot win this war without firing a shot. This is a life and death battle, and you need all your weapons, power and authority to be active. *"Ye are of God, little children, and have overcome them: because greater is he that is in you, than he that is in the world"* (1 John 4:4).

You have more authority than you think!!! Fight in the Spirit for your marriage! Fight in the Spirit for your children! Take spiritual authority over the addictions that would steal your loved ones! Anoint every doorpost in your home with oil and command every unclean spirit and demonic force to leave your home in Jesus' name! Memorize every scripture promise that relates to your particular situation and start praying that scripture! Get radical in the Spirit! Remember, your fight is not against flesh and blood. The fight has already been won on the cross! You just have to believe it and declare it!

When we were still living in Memphis, Tennessee, I had an experience that really solidified my faith in this area. I had been working with a local pastor in the inner city to help build a halfway house for men coming out of prison. I had not seen this pastor for several days, so on my lunch break I drove by his church to check on him. I tried several doors, but they were all locked so I started to walk off when suddenly the pastor opened one of the locked doors, reached out and grabbed my arm and pulled me inside this small room that he was in. When I got inside, I quickly learned that he was in the middle of ministering to a demon-possessed man from South America who had been heavily involved in the occult.

First of all, I was a fairly new Christian and would not have entered that room if I knew what was going on. However, God had other plans. To tell you the truth, I did not know what to do except pray. I did not know what to pray in English so I started praying in the Spirit. Almost immediately I heard the Lord tell me to quit praying and to speak to this demonic spirit and tell it to leave.

So, in my untrained, non-religious, and simple but very firm faith, I spoke to this spirit and basically said this: "I know who you are, and you know who I am, and we are not staying in the same room together. You have to go in Jesus' name!" Well, thanks be to God, it worked! The man got set free, but that is not the end of the story.

When I left that place and started driving home, I heard this voice in my head say, "Who do you think you are saying, 'I know who you are, and you know who I am'?" Thank God I had put enough Word in me by this time to be able to deal with this situation. The scripture that immediately came to my mind was Acts 19:11-15 where the seven sons of Sceva were trying to cast out demons. Do you remember the demon's response? He said, *"Jesus I know, and Paul I know; but who are you?"* (v. 15). This will change your life, just like it did mine, if you will really hear it. The demon did not just know Jesus. He knew Paul also, a born-again, Spirit-filled believer just like you and me!!

The demon did not just know Jesus. He knew Paul also, a born-again, Spirit-filled believer just like you and me!!

Satan will always try to convince you that you have no authority. Your job is to know the Word of God well enough to detect those lies and remind him who you are and whose you are. You have more authority than you think!!

One of the challenges I faced after being born again was X-rated dreams. As a heathen, I had watched all kinds of pornography. The enemy will replay those images over and over in your mind if you let him. I thought, like many of you probably think, *dreams are just dreams and there is nothing I can do about it.* Well, you are wrong! When I started to understand the power and authority that God had given us, I finally realized what the enemy was doing in my dreams and I started taking authority over my dreams.

I will never forget the night one of these dreams started, and in my sleep I took authority over the dream, and said, "In the name of Jesus, I will not dream this dream!" Do you know what happened? The dream ceased, I woke up and I never dreamed those dreams again. You have more authority than you think!

Cheryl's Insights

Soon after moving to the Memphis area, I was invited to a prayer meeting at the home of a local doctor. By this time I was singing and would go anywhere someone would let me sing. I went with my friend and they invited me to sing. After a time of music and praise and worship, I noticed that these people were very different. As the speaker began to preach and share the Word, I was blown away!

I had never heard the things he was preaching. He was telling us that we were overcomers, that God wanted to bless us, heal us and that we had power by the Holy Spirit to take authority over the enemy. I had never heard these things in the church I grew up in.

When he finished, I went up to the front and sneaked a peek at his Bible to see if it was like mine. It was the same Bible I had! Where did he get that stuff? Now these people were raising their hands, clapping, full of joy and speaking in some other language. This worried me, because I did not want to get mixed up with some crazies and end up in a ditch somewhere.

Our pastor was in some of these meetings so I went to him and asked him, "What is going on? Either these people are crazy or they have something I don't have. Which is it?" He could have told me this long thing about the book of Acts, but instead he said, "Why don't you just pray and ask God to show you?" That sounded good to me, so I prayed and said, "Lord, I don't understand what these people are doing, but if they have something I don't have and if it is from You, I want it! I want all You have for me, but God, don't let me get mixed up with crazy people."

I went back to that meeting three more times. On the third time, we were all gathered in a circle praying for one of the ladies who was going through some marital problems. As we were praying for her, I felt something stirring in me. I opened my mouth and began to speak in another language. My head was telling me to shut up, you are making a fool of yourself, be quiet, but my spirit was free and the language just poured out like the scripture says. Out of your belly will flow rivers of living water (John 7:38). When the prayer was finished, I turned to the lady next to me, and said, "I think I just spoke in tongues." She responded, "It's about time, I have been praying for you for three weeks!"

My walk with the Lord was forever changed. Now I understand Acts 1:8. Now I understand how to fight spiritual battles. Now I understand how to pray without ceasing. Now I understand how to pray when you don't know what to pray. There is so much more to the God we serve. He is exciting, wonderful and He wants to pour into us all He is. All we have to do is be willing to receive it. I never knew I could have the things I have received.

That was the beginning of an evangelistic ministry that started in Jerusalem (our home town) and spread to the United States and several other countries. You truly do have more authority than you think.

"Thou believest that there is one God; thou doest well: the devils also believe, and tremble" (James 2:19).

"And from the days of John the Baptist until the present time, the kingdom of heaven has endured violent assault, and violent [mighty] men seize it by force [as a precious prize—a share in the heavenly kingdom is sought with most ardent zeal and intense exertion]" (Matthew 11:12 AMP).

"And when he had called unto him his twelve disciples, he gave them power against unclean spirits, to cast them out, and to heal all manner of sickness and all manner of disease" (Matthew 10:1).

Chapter 7

Divine Appointments

God knows exactly what you need and He will bring the right people across your path at the perfect time. They may or may not have a title, and may not be exactly what you are expecting, but they will be the right people. When you have experienced a divine appointment, you will love God even more because you realize He is always working on your behalf. You just have to believe it and be on alert for those God-arranged meetings.

I will never forget a testimony I heard years ago from a famous evangelist. This man was a well-known and powerful speaker who had ministered all over the world and written many books. He said he was at the pinnacle of his ministry, and he had been praying for over a year about a particular personal situation and could not get an answer from God.

One weekend, he was ministering in a small church and had preached several times. He had finished praying for a multitude of people at the altar that night and was exhausted. He was one of the last to leave the church that night, except for a cleaning lady who was mopping the floor.

As he started to leave, the cleaning lady approached him. She was not very well dressed and in his mind he thought, *I do not have the time or the energy to minister to one more person.* As the lady approached him, she asked, in broken English, if she could spend a minute with him. He learned later that she was an immigrant from Poland. The evangelist reluctantly agreed to stop and hear what was on her mind.

As the slovenly dressed Polish woman stood before the well-dressed and renowned man of God, she began to prophesy to him in broken English. What she prophesied to this evangelist was the answer he had been seeking from God for over a year. It changed his life and his ministry forever.

"Let brotherly love continue. Be not forgetful to entertain [be hospitable to] *strangers: for thereby some have entertained* [hosted] *angels unawares"* (Hebrews 13:1-2).

We were working on a halfway house for prisoners in Memphis, Tennessee, and needed forty to fifty gallons of paint to help renovate this old building. We did not have the money for the paint and were getting a little discouraged.

As I was driving to work early one morning, I stopped at a red light that I had stopped at hundreds of times before. All of a sudden I looked to my left and there was a brightly blinking sign over this store that caught my attention. The sign was for a paint store, and I had never noticed that store or that sign before this particular morning.

As I looked at the sign, the Lord said to me, "This is where you get your paint." I had never heard God quite like that before, and questions flooded into my mind. Did I just hear God? Was that God or me?

I went on to work that morning, but that incident and what I heard would not leave me. Finally, I decided that I had to follow up on this to see whether this was God or not, but I first had to get past all the negative thoughts, such as, *You are going to look like a fool.*

At lunchtime I left work and went to this paint store. I shared what happened at the stoplight with the sales clerk in the paint store and he looked at me like I was from a different planet. He told me I would have to talk to the owner of the store and his office was in a different location out by the Memphis airport, which was several miles away. By this time I had to return to work.

The negative thoughts came flooding in again. *See, you did not hear God. You are just making a fool out of yourself.* Now I had to make the next decision. Am I going to try to talk to the owner? The next day I decided to go to the owner's airport office and tell him my story. When I arrived, the owner's secretary told me he was in a big board meeting but I could wait. So I waited for about an hour. You can imagine the thoughts that were telling me I was a fool and I should just get up and leave.

After an hour, the secretary said the owner was still tied up and maybe I should just tell her my story, so I did. I told her exactly what happened at the stoplight and what we needed the paint for. She calmly took down notes and at the end of our conversation she said she would call me after talking to the owner. I then left her office with the thoughts, *She will never call me. I probably did not hear God.*

The next afternoon I was in my office and a phone call came in for me. It was the owner's secretary. She said she had talked to the owner and he said for me to come to their warehouse and they would donate all the paint we needed. Do you have any idea what that did for my faith? Do you have any idea what that did for my love of God? God is not a respecter of persons, so whatever He did for me He will do for you also.

"Eye hath not seen, nor ear heard, neither have entered into the heart of man, the things that God hath prepared for them that love him" (1 Corinthians 2:9).

Cheryl and I were invited to attend the grand opening and ribbon cutting ceremonies for the INSP Television Network's new "City of Light" that opened in Indian Land, South Carolina, just south of Charlotte, North Carolina. This is a magnificent ministry center that David and Barbara Cerullo and The Inspiration Network built to broadcast the Gospel to the world.

As Cheryl and I walked into the live television broadcast with all the many ministry dignitaries, we were ushered to the front row with our son Chip Henderson and his wife Becky Cerullo Henderson and our two grandsons, Samuel and Matthew.

As we sat down on that front row, I was reminded that it was God who had put us in this position of ministry, not we ourselves, and we do not take that lightly. It is a gift of grace that we never could have imagined twenty-eight years ago when I gave my life to the Lord. I could have never imagined even being in the ministry at all, much less in the position that we are in. We could have never imagined a son and his family serving the Lord. Similarly, we could have never imagined being close friends with very prominent and successful business people and heads of ministries. We also could have never imagined writing this book.

But as I look back on our journey with the Lord and reflect on scripture, there are several promises of God that have come alive in our lives that are a direct result of just loving God and walking with Him. These same promises are for you also.

"Do you see a man diligent and skillful in his business? He will stand before kings; he will not stand before obscure men" (Proverbs 22:29 AMP).

"And the LORD shall make thee the head, and not the tail; and thou shalt be above only, and thou shalt not be beneath; if that thou hearken unto the commandments of the LORD thy God, which I command thee this day, to observe and to do them" (Deuteronomy 28:13).

"But God, who is rich in mercy, because of His great love with which He loved us, even when we were dead in trespasses, made us alive together with Christ (by grace you have been saved), and raised us up together, and made us sit together in the heavenly places in Christ Jesus, that in the ages to come He might show the exceeding riches of His grace in His kindness toward us in Christ Jesus. For by grace you have been saved through faith, and that not

of yourselves; it is the gift of God, not of works, lest anyone should boast" (Ephesians 2:4-9 NKJV).

Cheryl's Insights

Early on in our ministry, the Lord started putting people in our path to minister to. It was like we attracted them. I never felt like I had what it took to help them, but God kept sending them.

I had a girlfriend who told me that she was having an affair with another man who lived in our neighborhood. My girlfriend and the other man were both married and they both had children. Ed and I knew both spouses and all the children would play at our house from time to time. My heart sank as she told me what was going on. My response to her was, "Break it off right now. This will not end well, and this is a lie from the enemy. This will devastate both families." She would not heed my advice.

After several weeks, the whole situation was exposed. Our little town was buzzing with the gossip. Both families were in turmoil. My friend's husband left her and filed for divorce. The other man's wife left him, but soon returned to try to make it work. My friend was hurt, embarrassed, humiliated and depressed. I can remember that the other man and his wife would go for walks together right by my girlfriend's house, which caused even further pain. What a mess this was!

One day while doing household chores, I could not get my girlfriend off of my mind. I gave her a call, but the line was busy. I called several more times, but still the line was busy. After a little while, I went outside to hang out clothes. As I looked across the backyards to my girlfriend's home, I saw her ex-husband driving into her driveway. I heard the audible voice of God say, "GO!" Without hesitation, I dropped the clothes and ran across the backyards as fast as I could.

When I got to her house, her ex-husband was breaking a window to get into the house. Not a word was spoken between him and me. As he opened the door, we found her sitting up in a chair, slumped over with the phone in her lap. She was blue and cold. She had tried to commit suicide by taking an overdose of pills. Her ex-husband went to the phone and called 911. All I knew to do was grab her in my arms and speak out, "Devil, you will not have her!" Then I held her in my arms rocking back and forth praying in tongues!!

I knew I was in spiritual warfare for her life. There were no English words I could utter that would shake Heaven and hell. I was so thankful that I could pray in the Spirit and know that it was a perfect prayer that went straight to the throne room.

After only a few minutes, the paramedics got there and rushed her to the hospital. The doctor said that if we had been a few minutes longer finding her, she would have died. But she didn't die!! Now she and her husband never reconciled, and I don't know where she is today. But I do know that God's Word works, and He equips us for what He calls us to do. I know that spiritual warfare is done in the Spirit and that speaking in tongues has a divine purpose in our lives and is part of God's armor.

"Wherefore take unto you the whole armour of God, that ye may be able to withstand in the evil day, and having done all, to stand. Stand therefore, having your loins girt about with truth, and having on the breastplate of right-eousness; and your feet shod with the preparation of the gospel of peace; above all, taking the shield of faith, wherewith ye shall be able to quench all the fiery darts of the wicked. And take the helmet of salvation, and the sword of the Spirit, which is the word of God: Praying always with all prayer and supplication in the Spirit, and watching thereunto with all perseverance and supplica-tion for all saints" (Ephesians 6:13-18).

God will put people in your path that you never imag-ined. He arranges divine appointments, such as Jesus with the woman at the well; Ananias with Paul at Damascus; Peter and John with the lame man at the Gate called Beautiful; or you and me with the right people for our business or ministry. Our responsibility is to love God, stay ready, be alert and go. Just remember, two-thirds of God's name is "GO."

Just remember, two-thirds of God's name is "GO."

Lord, we pray for divine appoint-ments for everyone reading this chapter. We know that Your will is for all of us to prosper and be in health. Help us, Lord, to be attentive to Your voice and to the leading of Your Spirit. Thank You for Your gift of grace that makes our weak-nesses strong and gives us the boldness to go.

Chapter 8
Your Seed Shall Be Mighty

"Praise ye the Lord. Blessed is the man that feareth the Lord, that delighteth greatly in his commandments. His seed shall be mighty upon earth: the generation of the upright shall be blessed. Wealth and riches shall be in his house: and his righteousness endureth for ever" (Psalm 112:1-4).

What an awesome promise! Sounds to me like God's heart is for you and me and our children to prosper! However, the secret to inheriting the promises is to line up with the conditions. The conditions in this case include fearing (respecting and loving) the Lord, delighting ourselves in the Word of God and sowing seed. In today's fast food society, we always want things instantly. However, in God's society, most things are a process (line upon line). God can still do instant miracles, but most things involve a process.

First, there needs to be a respect (love) and reverence (fear) for the things of God. That takes humility, getting to the end of ourselves and recognizing that we need God's help.

Secondly, after we have humbled ourselves before God, we need to delight ourselves in the Word of God. Most people do not have a clue how powerful the Word of God is. The Bible is not just a religious book. It is quick (alive) and powerful and able to discern the thoughts and the intents of our hearts. It can change our thinking! It can give us supernatural wisdom and guidance! It can save us and give us eternal life! It can heal our bodies! It can provide answers for us that no other source can!

But the key to receiving any of this is that we need to read it. That is the first way that we show respect and love.

If a rich relative left a lengthy will that was full of gifts to be disbursed between certain family members, including yourself, would you not read it? I bet you would read every word to make sure you obtained your portion of that inheritance. How much more should you know what your inheritance is from God!

Cheryl's Insights

Raising three boys has been, to use the old quote, "The best of times and the worst of times." We have had opportunity to stand on every promise God gave us for our seed, and God has always been faithful. I don't think anyone has any idea of how precious, wondrous and challenging a child is until you have had one of your own.

When our youngest son, Chip, was five years old, we were riding down the road and he asked me how you get to go to Heaven. I explained the best I could what it meant to be born again and filled with the Holy Spirit. He said, "I want to do that right now!" So while driving down the road in Memphis, Tennessee, that sweet, innocent child asked Jesus into his heart and asked to be filled with the Holy Spirit.

That was my first glimpse of what Jesus meant when He said to come to Him as a child. As Chip prayed, he just believed that God would do His part. He believed that he would go to Heaven one day, and he believed that the Holy Spirit would fill him completely. It was that simple. Chip did not speak in tongues at that moment, but I knew that God had filled him and that in time Chip would manifest his prayer language.

A few days later, Chip and I were visiting our pastor and his wife at their home. While we were there, it started to snow and the roads started to ice over. I told Chip that we needed to get back home before the roads became too icy to drive. As we were driving home, I realized that the roads had already become dangerous. About that time I hit a patch of ice, and I said, "Chip, you need to pray right now! I don't want to end up in a ditch!"

How faithful God is to move in our lives at just the right time.

Without hesitation, he started to pray . . . in tongues!!! It so shocked me that I almost ran into the ditch without the help of the ice!!! How faithful God is to move in our lives at just the right time.

How faithful He is to answer the prayer of a five-year-old child to be filled with His precious Holy Spirit.

Did you know that your spirit man is the part of you that will live forever! In the spirit, there is no age limit, no gender limit, no limit whatsoever, except what you put on it!! God is able to do exceedingly abundantly more than you can ask or think!!

There were other times in raising our sons that were hard, heartbreaking, and quite frankly embarrassing. As one of our sons entered his teenage years, we dealt with rebellion, drugs, illegal activity and eventually jail. The enemy jumped right on us with doubt, condemnation and fear. As parents, the enemy always tries to convince you that you are a failure as a parent and that whatever your child gets into that is bad is all your fault. You must have done something or failed to do something to cause this child to go that way.

So many negative thoughts flooded our minds, especially this one: "Some kind of preachers you two are, and your own son is in jail." Those were tough times and I don't ever want to go through them again. However, God is always faithful and He watches over His Word to perform it in our lives. His promises have come to pass for all our children (including the one who was in jail), and they are all safe, born again and living good lives. We now have seven grandchildren.

As we went through those tough periods, the only person that we could rely on and trust in was God, and He gave us two scriptures that we stood on. The first scripture was Proverbs 11:21 that says, *"The seed of the righteous shall be delivered."* We locked onto that promise and would not let go!! The second scripture was Isaiah 1:2 that says, *"Hear, O heavens, and give ear, O earth; for the Lord hath spoken, I have nourished and brought up children, and they have rebelled against me."*

Wow! Even God, the perfect parent, had rebellious children. I can't begin to tell you how that set us free from condemnation. If you have a prodigal out there, take these scriptures for your own and don't let go.

I will never forget a family prayer session we had one night in our home. Cheryl and I and the boys were all gathered together in our den for a devotional and family prayer. We were ministering on the road in prisons and churches and our family car was getting old. The car had over 100,000 miles on it, and we did not have enough space to haul all the sound equipment we were using. We needed a van.

As we prayed that night, our youngest son addressed God like he always did, very bluntly. He said, "Lord, we need a van. And by the way, make it a red van. And make sure it has tires on it. Thank You, Lord." We all sort of snickered, but our son was serious.

We had looked for vans for several weeks and could not find anything that fit our needs or our pocketbook. Then one night we were riding around and decided to stop at a GMC dealer to see what they might have. It was raining and we had almost given up by this time of finding what we needed.

Our son jumped out of the car and ran off looking at cars while Cheryl and I went to talk to the salesman. The salesman told us that he had just got a van in that very day that may be what we were looking for. About that time our son came running up to us, yelling, "I found it, I found it!" It was the van the salesman had told us about. It was a red van, and it had tires on it!

Do you know what that did for our son's faith and his love of God, not to mention what it did for us? We drove that van over 100,000 miles and ministered in hundreds of places, and we never snickered at our son's prayers anymore.

Finally, seed is a big key to prosperity! "Seed" in the context of Psalm 112 not only refers to our children (which it does), but it also refers to the finances that we sow. Verse 5 of Psalm 112 describes a good man as one who lends, and verse 9 says that he has dispersed and given to the poor. Your seed is mighty!!!

The definition for the Hebrew word for "mighty" in Psalm 112 includes "victory," "warrior," and "go to war." The victory is in the seed that you sow! The battle is waged with the seed that you sow! The war is fought with the seed that you sow! But seed is worthless if not planted.

One of our former Sunday school teachers in Memphis, Tennessee, had a saying that has always stuck with us over the years. That saying was, "The victory is not in the fight but in the surrender." We pass that on to you today. Surrender to God, respect (love) the things of God, delight yourself in the Word of God, sow bountifully, pray for your children and lock into God's promises concerning them, and your house and your children will prosper!

"The victory is not in the fight but in the surrender."

Chapter 9

Keys to Success

There are literally thousands of "SUCCESS" books on the market advising you how to be a success in everything from your marriage to your business. Cheryl and I have spent the last twenty years working and serving with some very successful business and ministry people, and until just recently, I was never able to summarize in words the key ingredients that I felt contributed to these individual successes.

Recently, I was watching a television documentary on Olympic gold medal winners and what they individually had to go through to reach the pinnacle of success in their particular sports. The commentator was describing a story of two Scandinavian brothers who had endured all manner of setbacks, including major injuries, which would have crippled normal people. But these brothers kept after it year after year and even at an older age were able to win gold medals at the Winter Olympics.

At the end of the documentary, the commentator used a quote from Claude T. Bissell, the late President of the

University of Toronto, to depict the attitudes that he felt best described these particular Olympians. This quote is the best description I have ever heard of the attitude and spirit that I have witnessed in the super successful:

> They risk more than others think is safe.
>
> They care more than others think is wise.
>
> They dream more than others think is practical.
>
> They expect more than others think is possible.

Cheryl's Insights

When Ed and I gave our lives to the Lord back in the 1980's we knew that we wanted to do something important for the Kingdom of God. We did not want to just sit in a church pew and go through the same ole, same ole.

In 1989, we moved to Jacksonville, Florida, and there we met Brig and Lita Hart. When Brig shared his vision with us for a ministry called New Life Network, we were very skeptical at first. Here was a man working in a network-marketing arena that we literally hated. Surely God was not in this type of business. But Brig encouraged us to come to one of his meetings and just take a look for ourselves, so we agreed.

We went with him as his guests to Knoxville, Tennessee, to a meeting that had over 20,000 network marketers in attendance. On Sunday morning, they had a voluntary church service. At the end of that service, they had an altar call and over 1,000 people gave their lives to the Lord. My husband and I stood backstage and just cried. We had no idea this mission field even existed.

We told God that morning we would do whatever He wanted us to do and that was the start of a ministry that has spanned over twenty years and has resulted in 5,000 to 10,000 people a year being born again.

I started New Life Network in a little office with one desk, one phone and one computer and printer. It took me hours just to figure out how to put paper in the printer!!! And we were going to do great things for God . . .Yeah! Right!

I will never forget our first business function as we began serving as Chaplains for Brig's organization. We had this six-foot table with one book. All the other speakers' tables were loaded with material. Listen to me! Don't ever despise small beginnings! The one book that we had was a great book entitled *Prayers That Avail Much*. It was that book that helped teach me how to pray.

We didn't look very impressive, but we had a dream in our hearts and a calling on our lives. We knew that this was what we were supposed to be doing. Today, we carry hundreds of books, CDs, Bibles, music, etc. From our book table at major business functions to our web site, it is all about ministering to people and their families. It has taken over twenty years for God to do in us and through us what He has wanted to do from the beginning, and it is not over yet!!

We have taken a lot of criticism and even lost a few relationships, including pastors, along the way. We had plenty of people telling us why it wouldn't work and why we should not be associated with these people. There have been, and will always be, plenty of naysayers along the way. "The risk is too high," they will say! "Business is not the place for ministry," they will say! "You are just dreaming," they will say! "This will never work," they will say! "Be practical," they will say! "You are going to offend people with this Jesus stuff," they will say! And on and on and on!!! This is when your love for God and people needs to be stronger than all the naysayers.

I love the scripture in 1 Corinthians 2:9: "Your eye has not seen it, nor have you heard it. Honey, you can't even think how wonderful the things are that God has prepared for those who love Him" (Cheryl's version).

I will never forget a lesson God taught us years ago. Ed was lying on the couch in our home one weekend watching a drag race on television. I walked through the den several times that afternoon and would glance at the television. Later on in the afternoon, I walked through the den and I noticed fire coming out of the exhaust of one of the cars that was drag racing. I stopped and asked Ed, "What was that?" because I had not seen that fire before. He told me that the fire was always there, but we could not see it because it was not dark enough outside. As it started to get dark, you could all of a sudden see the flames.

You need to go to the dark places to see His power manifested.

God spoke to us through that drag race. His power is just like that. You need to go to the dark places to see His power manifested. That is exactly what we have seen over the years in the business world where people who have never been in a church will come to a meeting to hear about building a business, but would never go to a church. That is where you see the power of God move.

We encourage you to press in to the love of God, the presence of God and the power of God, and watch God do His thing. Take His Word to the dry and barren places and watch miracles happen!

We have a ministry acquaintance (Rodney Howard-Browne) who was given a dream by God in 1998 to have an evangelistic service in New York City. In the summer of 1999, his ministry rented Madison Square Garden for six weeks to conduct this crusade. Can you just imagine the costs (millions) involved? Can you just imagine the people who told him that this was a very foolish idea? There was a lot of resistance to his God idea.

If you look at the videos of some of those meetings, you will see footage of a service where Rodney told the audience prophetically (in 1999) that there were people in foreign lands planning for their destruction at that very minute. He asked the audience at one point what they would do if a missile were to hit the middle of New York City.

Looking at those videos now will send chills down your spine. Do you recall what happened on September 11, 2001? Thousands of people lost their lives as two jets, piloted by foreign terrorists, flew into the Twin Towers. I hope we all never forget. But listen to this. You never heard about this earlier crusade on any news program. Over 48,000 people gave their hearts to Jesus at those meetings held at Madison Square Garden in the summer of 1999, and I would bet some of those same people probably lost their lives on 9/11/2001. What caused Rodney to do such an apparent outlandish thing? It was his extravagant love of God!!!

Dream big and never let anyone talk you out of or steal your dreams.

If you want to be successful in anything, you are going to have to take some risks. It is never unwise to care. Dream big and never let anyone talk you out of or steal your dreams. Expect the best. You only go through this life one time. We made the decision twenty years ago that we did not want to be eighty or ninety years of age and look back on our life with regrets that we did not attempt to do what we thought God had called us to do and trusted Him to provide. I sure am glad we made that decision, and Cheryl and I can report to you today that God has never let us down.

We had a close female friend in Memphis that was an African-American evangelist. She was on fire for Jesus and was a preaching machine. She was also a supervisor at the main post office in downtown Memphis. She called us one day and told us she had been asked to be President of a women's organization that was comprised of women in federal employment who were in management positions. She wanted Cheryl and me to help her swear in the new officers, including her, and pray over this organization, which we gladly agreed to do.

At the beginning of the meeting, our friend addressed the audience. I will never forget what she told that group of very influential women. This particular group had obviously had some organizational problems in the past and she confronted that straight on. She told them that she basically viewed this organization as dead due to all the past problems they had experienced. She told them that there are only two things you can do with something that is dead. You can either bury it, or you can resurrect it. She told them, "I am here to resurrect this from the dead!" It was a powerful statement and an attitude that I have never forgotten. We are in the resurrection business!

There is just one more item I would add to describe the nature and attitude of the super successful, especially in a ministry position. They are quick to forgive. It was the super religious that Jesus had the most problems with. It has not changed much over the years. There is a scripture that has been very beneficial to me over the years when people have lied about us, stolen from us, judged us, accused us or just plain hurt us. That scripture is in Hebrews 12:3-4 which says, *"For consider him that endured such contradiction of sinners against himself, lest ye be wearied and faint in your minds. Ye have not yet resisted unto blood, striving against sin."*

Regardless of what anybody does, you and I have not hung on a cross and suffered the brutality that Jesus suffered, and He said, "Forgive them, Father, for they know not what they do." When you compare what you are going through to what Jesus went through, it helps put things in perspective and will help you forgive quicker.

"Be strong (confident) and of good courage, for you shall cause this people to inherit the land which I swore to their fathers to give them. Only you be strong and very courageous, that you may do according to all the law which Moses my servant commanded you. Turn not from it to the right hand or to the left, that you may prosper wherever you go. This Book of the Law shall not depart out of your mouth, but you shall meditate on it day and night, that you may observe and do according to all that is written in it. For then you shall make your way prosperous, and then you shall deal wisely and have good success" (Joshua 1:6-8 AMP).

"Now unto him that is able to do exceeding abundantly above all that we ask or think, according to the power that worketh in us" (Ephesians 3:20).

Chapter 10

When a Storm Hits, You Need a Friend

Several years ago, Cheryl and I had to evacuate our home in Orange Park, Florida, due to the threat of Hurricane Floyd. We spent several days with some very special friends in Lake City, Florida. Thank the Lord for good friends who are always there in hard times. We love you, Charlie and Debbie!

There are all types of hurricanes. This one was named Floyd, but yours may be called divorce, or bankruptcy, or abuse, or addiction, or sickness, or depression, or loneliness, or debt or a multitude of other storms that blow through our lives. Hurricanes have basically one purpose: to kill, steal and destroy. Sounds like a verse I read in John 10:10. But Jesus comes to give us life and life more abundantly, and friends can be a critical part of that solution.

The scripture says, *"Two are better than one; because they have a good reward for their labour. For if they fall, the one will lift up his fellow: but woe to him that is alone when he falleth; for he hath not another to help him up"* (Ecclesiastes 4:9-10).

Sometimes we need some flesh and bone to touch us, help us, love us, pray with us, agree with us or just say, "Everything is going to be all right."

I know that many of us "Word" people would say to just stand strong and believe the Word of God. There is nothing wrong with that, but sometimes we need a friend. Sometimes we need some flesh and bone to touch us, help us, love us, pray with us, agree with us or just say, "Everything is going to be all right."

The Bible describes a friend in Proverbs 17:17 as one that *"loveth at all times."* Do you have a friend who sticks with you through all your faults, all your weaknesses, through the bad and the ugly? If you do, thank the Lord every day! If you don't, let me tell you about One who sticks closer than a brother. His name is JESUS!!! The Bible says He will never leave you or forsake you. Can you imagine that? Regardless of what you do, if you have asked Jesus into your heart, He will not run at the first sound of trouble. He will not hide when you are going through a battle. You can always call on Him and He will never disappoint you.

Cheryl and I recently celebrated our forty-second wedding anniversary with these same special friends, Charlie and Debbie, at their new and magnificent home in Holmes Beach, Florida, on Anna Maria Island. On the last day that we were in Florida, Charlie decided we would go tarpon fishing since he knew I loved to fish. He hired two young guides, and we left at 6:30 a.m. to search for these magnificent silver fish.

It didn't take long, after catching the baitfish, to locate a school of tarpon. It was some sight to see these beautiful fish breaking the water as they swam in large schools. I was the first to catch one that weighed about 85 pounds and it took forty-five minutes to get it to the boat. These fish are very strong and determined.

At one point into this very tiring fight, Charlie had to grab me by the belt to steady me. It is always helpful to have somebody alongside you to help when you are in a struggle. We eventually got the tarpon to the side of the boat and released it unharmed. I never caught a fish that fought like that.

A little while later, Charlie hooked a giant tarpon that was a lot bigger than mine, and he was in for the fight of his life with this fish. Every time it looked like Charlie was gaining a little ground, this tarpon would make a strong run back away from the boat to his school. One of our young guides kept saying, "He just will not leave that school." After fighting this fish for one hour and fifteen minutes, the line broke and the tarpon went free. Needless to say, Charlie was very tired and at points in that battle, I had to grab him by the belt and steady him, just as he had done for me.

What an awesome picture this episode shows of the power of love, friendship, encouragement and unity. I am not just referring to Charlie and myself, but also to the tarpon and his buddies. I can just imagine the other tarpon in that school encouraging the one with the hook in his mouth. They were encouraging him, with their presence and actions, to not give up. They could have abandoned the one that was hooked, but they did not. They were actually a protection and an encouragement for him and eventually were probably the main reason that he got free.

There are a lot of people out there with a hook in their mouth, and they need to see and be around successful, godly encouragers. They need to know that freedom is possible if they hang around the right crowd and just don't give up.

There is a scripture in Joel 2:7 that talks about a great army. It says, *"They shall run like mighty men; they shall climb the wall like men of war; and they shall march every one on his ways, and they shall not break their ranks."* There is just something about the safety and anointing of a group of people who have joined together for a single purpose and are following the commands and love of the Lord. Sounds to me like what the Body of Christ (the Church) is supposed to be about. Sounds to me like what our relationship with the Lord is to be about.

Learn the lesson of the tarpon. Just keep running towards freedom, keep running with the right crowd, keep running with and loving God, and eventually any hook will come out and freedom will come.

Our home in Southwest Georgia is surrounded by huge, majestic pine trees, which are very prevalent in this area. They create a beautiful setting for a home, until the storms come. Afternoon thunderstorms, with their heavy rain and high winds, are very common in the hot and humid summers of South Georgia. As the winds blow and the rain pours, the pine trees shed their limbs and their pine cones all over manicured lawns, and we, along with our neighbors, gather them up and place them in large piles for burning.

I spend about every other day in the summer gathering limbs and pine cones from my front and backyard after late afternoon thunderstorms. It has become apparent during these cleanup sessions that most of the debris that has succumbed to the storms is withered limbs and dead pine cones. You hardly ever find a live limb (full of sap) or a green pine cone that has been blown away. It takes a really, really strong storm to break away a healthy limb or green pine cone.

Did you know that God refers to us as trees in the Bible on many occasions? Psalm 1:3 says, *"And he shall be like a tree planted by the rivers of water . . ."* (Also see Jeremiah 17:8.) Psalm 104:16 says, *"The trees of the Lord are full of sap. . . ."* Isaiah 61:3 says, *"That they might be called trees of righteousness, the planting of the Lord, that he might be glorified."*

In the days we live in, there are storms all around us. There are business storms, financial storms, relationship storms, family storms, political storms, ecological storms and every other type of storm you can think of. So how do we keep from being blown away? How do we weather these storms? The answer is that you have to have a firm foundation and stay full of sap!! You have to stay green!! You have to stay full of life!! You need a friend!!

Jesus said it best in John 15:5-7: *"I am the vine, ye are the branches. He that abideth in me, and I in him, the same bringeth forth much fruit; for without me ye can do nothing. If a man abide not in me, he is cast forth as a branch, and is withered; and men gather them, and cast them into the fire, and they are burned. If ye abide in me, and my words abide in you, ye shall ask what ye will, and it shall be done unto you."*

Years ago, I heard a great teaching on the date palm tree that grows in the deserts of Africa. In this teaching, they talked about how each time the strong winds of a desert storm would come, the date palm tree would bend a little. But what happened below the surface, out of sight, was that the roots would be loosened just enough to give the date palm the opportunity to sink deeper and deeper roots, thereby making it stronger and stronger.

We encourage each of you today to stay plugged into the vine. Stay full of sap. If someone were to come and check your Word dipstick, let it always read full. Do not let the storms of life blow you over and cast you forth like a withered branch or a dead pine cone. Let the storms make you stronger and stronger. Sink your roots deeper and deeper into God and His Word, and as you do this, your love for God will grow more and more.

"My brethren, count it all joy when ye fall into divers temptations [tests, trials, experiences], knowing this, that the trying [proving, testing] of your faith worketh patience [leads to steadfastness, develops endurance, breeds fortitude]. But let patience have her perfect work, that ye may be perfect and entire [mature and complete, fully developed and perfectly equipped], wanting nothing [in nothing coming short, in no respect deficient]" (James 1:2-4).

"A friend loveth at all times, and a brother is born for adversity" (Proverbs 17:17).

"Iron sharpeneth iron; so a man sharpeneth the countenance of his friend" (Proverbs 27:17).

"I will not leave you comfortless: I will come to you" (John 14:18).

"I will never leave thee, nor forsake thee" (Hebrews 13:5).

Chapter 11
We Hope You Always Dance with God

I never want to leave the impression with anyone that everything comes up roses when you give your life to the Lord and start walking with Him. There will be hard times, disappointments and challenges. You can count on it (John 16:33). But you will always have some very close friends who will walk with you through each situation to give you strength and wisdom. That would be God the Father, God the Son (Jesus), God the Holy Spirit and a host of angels. You cannot go wrong with that crowd.

I have never been a huge country music fan, but every now and then a country song will come along that speaks to me in a very special way. "I Hope You Dance," written by Mark D. Sanders and Tia Sillers and sung by Lee Ann Womack, is one such song that touched and encouraged me. This song talks about how we respond to things in our life and that when we go through tough times to respond by dancing.

If you've been around very long at all, you have experienced some ups and downs. The scriptures tell us that in this world we will experience tribulation. We all suffer from time to time, but we should walk by faith and not by sight, knowing that we have the victory in Jesus Christ, and that nothing can separate us from the love of God.

Cheryl's Insights

Have you heard the saying, "Our life on earth is God's gift to us and what we do with that life is our gift to God"? You know, life is filled with choices. We can choose to say whatever we want, act the way we want and do the things we want, because God gives all of us a free will. You can choose to be happy or choose to be mad. You can choose to see the glass half empty or half full.

In the book of Deuteronomy, God says that He lays before us choices of life and death, blessing and cursing, but He wants us to choose life, that we and our household may prosper (Cheryl's paraphrase). The key is, we get to choose.

We had a precious doctor friend in Memphis who was a pediatrician. She loved children as well as having such a heart for teaching God's Word and for helping people. She worked at her practice half of the year, and the other half she took mission trips and spent a large part of her time in the Bush in Africa evangelizing the native people while helping them medically.

One day she called us and asked us to come over to her house and pray for her. She was really sick. She had been ill for several months and was unable to determine the cause. She just thought she was run down. (Sometimes doctors are the worst patients.) She had contracted malaria from her last trip to Africa. She told me that malaria is one of those diseases that can store in your body and release at some future time.

What she did not know was that on that day, Ed had some dental work done and his jaw was swollen up and he looked like a blowfish. I had been putting logs in our wood burning stove at home and the fumes came back in my face, and I had poison sumac all around my eyes. I looked like I had been in a fight with my eyes almost completely swollen shut.

When we arrived at her house, we all stumbled into her kitchen and started to share ministry stories. We wanted to get caught up on all the things the Lord had been doing in our lives and ministries. As we sat there chatting, Ed began to laugh. I said, "What is so funny?" He turned to us and said, "Look at us! Great men and women of faith . . . we look like we have all been run over by a freight train!" We each looked at the other, and then we all began to laugh!!!

The verse Ed spoke out as we sat there laughing at ourselves was James 1:2-4 NKJV: *"My brethren, count it all joy when you fall into various trials, knowing that the testing of your faith produces patience. But let patience have its perfect work, that you may be perfect and complete, lacking nothing."* From that moment, we were set free in the presence of the Lord and began to dance around that kitchen praising God and laughing.

If you had been there, you might have called the guys in the white coats. But you know, we left that house that night renewed and refreshed. Within a few days, we were all healed and back to normal doing what God had called us to do.

God's Word always works! We just have to be transparent enough to laugh at ourselves, not worry what others think and be real with God. Even if someone had put our little episode in the kitchen on U-Tube, I would not mind the world seeing me act foolish. I received healing in my body and the joy of the Lord was stirred up in me. We all know that it is the joy of the Lord that is our strength! I choose to always dance! I hope you do too!

I heard a testimony years ago about a fellow minister who was counseling with a pastor and his wife. This pastor and his wife had not taken a vacation from their church in years, so they decided to take their family on a two-week trip to rest and relax. When they returned from their vacation, they were stunned to learn that they had been voted out of their church. It was a devastating and unexpected event.

The minister who was counseling with this couple listened to all the circumstances and then asked them a question. His question to the pastor and his wife was, "How do you think you will look at this situation in ten or fifteen years?" As they thought about that question, the counselor offered some profound wisdom to this pastor and his wife that has always helped Cheryl and me through tough times.

The counselor said he believed that years down the road, we would look back on this event, and say, "You know when we went on vacation that one time and we returned home and had been voted out of our church position?" And we will all have a big laugh about it. And then the counselor said this: "If we are going to laugh about it somewhere in the future, let's just laugh about it now by faith." And that is exactly what they did.

"A merry heart doeth good like a medicine: but a broken spirit drieth the bones" (Proverbs 17:22).

Cheryl and I want to encourage you to always dance and laugh with God! In the midst of disappointment, DANCE and LAUGH with God! When the enemy whispers or yells in your ear that you are through or that you have missed it, DANCE and LAUGH with God! When your best friend, pastor, priest or prophet has let you down, DANCE and LAUGH with God! When you have lost your job and it looks like no one will ever hire you again, DANCE and LAUGH with God! When your heart is broken over a prodigal son or daughter, DANCE and LAUGH with God!

In the midst of every storm that comes your way, WE HOPE YOU DANCE AND LAUGH WITH GOD!

In the midst of every storm that comes your way, WE HOPE YOU DANCE AND LAUGH WITH GOD! He can change your life and circumstances with just one dance.

"Praise the Lord. Praise God in his sanctuary; praise him in his mighty heavens. Praise him for his acts of power; praise him for his surpassing greatness. Praise him with the sounding of the trumpet, praise him with the harp and lyre, praise him with tambourine and dancing, praise him with the strings and flute, praise him with the clash of cymbals, praise him with resounding cymbals. Let everything that has breath praise the LORD" (Psalm 150 NIV).

"And David danced before the Lord with all his might . . ." (2 Samuel 6:14).

Chapter 12

Never Give Up

One of the things Cheryl and I love to do together in our downtime is bass fish. We headed out one morning at 5:45, and as we were headed toward this beautiful lake, we decided to have a devotional on fishing. The following is a short synopsis of that devotional as we drove our truck and boat to the fishing hole.

Jesus chose fishermen as His first four disciples. *"And Jesus, walking by the sea of Galilee, saw two brethren, Simon called Peter, and Andrew his brother, casting a net into the sea: for they were fishers. And he saith unto them, Follow me, and I will make you fishers of men. And they straightway left their nets, and followed him. And going on from thence, he saw other two brethren, James the son of Zebedee, and John his brother, in a ship with Zebedee their father, mending their nets; and he called them. And they immediately left the ship and their father, and followed him"* (Matthew 4:18-22).

Jesus is still choosing regular people like you and me to accomplish miraculous things for the Kingdom of God.

His recruitment is not limited to the rich and well educated. When you realize this, it should make you love Him even more.

I started bass fishing with my dad when I was about ten years old, and I've learned a lot from fishing that applies to daily life and especially if you are in the ministry. An avid bass fisherman always understands that he is just one cast away from catching Oscar (that's what my dad called a big bass), regardless of how many nonproductive casts have been made in the past several hours.

There is a story in John 21 where Jesus appeared to His disciples who had been fishing all night, and He asked them if they had caught anything. They answered that they had not caught even one fish. He told them to cast on the other side of the boat, and when they did, they caught so many fish that they had to get help to haul them all in. These disciples had been fishing all night and were obviously discouraged.

What I want you to see here is that they were closer to success than they ever imagined. **They were just a few feet and one more cast away from a boatload of abundance.**

In our walk with the Lord, there have been times that looked very bleak, but we have always maintained that fisherman's faith that we were just one more cast away from a miracle. We just had to keep on casting.

We started bass fishing this particular day in this new South Georgia lake using a green plastic worm. After an hour of no action, I switched to a red worm and the first cast I made with that red worm, I caught a big bass. We caught several nice bass after that with that red worm. I have learned over the years that bass are very particular about what they will hit. Sometimes the smallest change, a different color, a different presentation, a different type lure or a different location is all you need to be successful.

It is the same way with fishing for men. If you are not having any success fishing for men, try changing your lure, change your presentation or try a different spot on the lake. Most importantly, ask the Lord where you should be fishing. Cheryl and I would have never imagined when we entered the ministry twenty-eight years ago that we would be fishing in the body of water that we are fishing in now. Jesus is the best fisherman ever, and He knows where you need to be fishing. His desire is for you to have a boatload of fish.

> *Jesus is the best fisherman ever, and He knows where you need to be fishing.*

There have been several major events along our fishing-for-men journey with God that have taught us significant lessons about the love of God. One such event happened in Memphis, Tennessee. A young man named George started attending our church and we quickly became close friends with this young man. He was the son of a very wealthy bank president in our city. He had spent most of his teenage years traveling the world and dabbling in all types of religions. When we met him, he had given his life to the Lord and he was just seeking more of God.

You see, George had cystic fibrosis and the doctors had told him that he would probably not live past his teenage years. George was twenty years old at this time, but every few months he would get really sick and have to spend several weeks in the hospital. Well, we were convinced that God would heal him, so we prayed fervently for George for two years. As we became closer with George, we learned that his main heart's desire was to see his entire family saved.

One weekend we received a call from his family that George was back in the hospital. He was not doing well at all and was not expected to live. My wife and I went to the hospital and met with the family and prayed for George. By this time he was comatose and had lost so much weight we could hardly recognize him. Later the next day, we were notified that George had passed away.

So many questions flooded our minds. God, why did You not heal George? He was too young to die. Did we do everything we could? Was there something else we could have done? Was our faith not strong enough?

Several weeks after George's funeral, his parents came to our church and asked our pastor if they could speak to the congregation. We had no idea what they wanted to say, but the pastor granted their request. The father started by saying that his son loved our church, and his father felt like he needed to share what happened the night George passed away. He said the entire family was in the hospital room and it was about 3:00 a.m. George had not spoken a word for several days and was still in a comatose state.

All of a sudden, George sat straight up in the bed, pointed to corner of the ceiling, and said, "I see it! It is so beautiful! I have the wisdom of Solomon right now. Somebody needs to ask me a question." The family was so stunned that no one asked a question. George lay back down on the hospital bed and went home to be with the Lord. After that incident, George's entire family gave their lives to the Lord. What a miracle! How do you think that affected our love for God?

God will always take what the enemy means for harm and turn it for good. George's sickness was from the enemy, not from God. In this one instance, we lost the battle for George's earthly life, but Satan lost the eternal war. George is walking the streets of gold today healed and his family is saved.

Our job is to be obedient to the Word that says we are to lay hands on the sick and pray for their healing. The results are in God's hands. I believe we are to fight sickness and disease with everything we have, which includes doctors, hospitals, medicine and prayer. We are in an army, and even though we lose one battle, that does not mean we abandon our position.

We have churches that are full of people who hear the message of salvation, but not all of those people will be saved. That does not mean you quit preaching salvation. Doctors are not able to save every patient, but that does not mean they quit being a doctor. If someone you pray for dies, that does not mean you quit praying. We are to never give up or back up!!!

We received a phone call shortly after this incident to consider coming to the women's prison in Memphis to minister to the women. The phone call was from an Indian Hindu lady who was in charge of the social programs at this institution. To this day we do not know how she got our names. We agreed to go and went on several occasions before moving from Memphis. Our Hindu host would always sit on the front row, and she would cry throughout our entire service.

One day as we were leaving the prison chapel, she pulled us aside and shared a personal story with us. She had recently been to her eye doctor for an examination and was told that she had a disease that would eventually make her blind. She requested we pray for her. By this time Cheryl and I were tired and we just wanted to get home. Neither one of us felt particularly holy or anointed. We laid hands on our Hindu host in the corridor of the jail and prayed a quick prayer for her healing and left the prison.

We did not see this Hindu lady for several weeks, but when we did see her, she said she had something very exciting she wanted to share with us. She said she had been back to her doctor and he could not find any sign of the disease. What do you think that did for our faith and for our love of God? We learned a great lesson from that incident. God is still in the miracle business, and He will use the most unusual situations to show those miracles. The absence of our pride and ego could have something to do with it. You and I just need to be obedient to the Word.

"But he was wounded for our transgressions, he was bruised for our iniquities: the chastisement of our peace was upon him; and with his stripes we are healed" (Isaiah 53:5).

"My son, attend to my words; incline thine ear unto my sayings. Let them not depart from thine eyes; keep them in the midst of thine heart. For they are life unto those that find them, and health to all their flesh" (Proverbs 4:20-22).

"For I will restore health unto thee, and I will heal thee of thy wounds, saith the Lord . . ." (Jeremiah 30:17).

"And Jesus went about all the cities and villages, teaching in their synagogues, and preaching the gospel of the kingdom, and healing every sickness and every disease among the people" (Matthew 9:35).

"How God anointed Jesus of Nazareth with the Holy Ghost and with power: who went about doing good, and healing all that were oppressed of the devil; for God was with him" (Acts 10:38).

"Is any sick among you? let him call for the elders of the church; and let them pray over him, anointing him with oil in the name of the Lord: And the prayer of faith shall save the sick, and the Lord shall raise him up; and if he hath committed sins, they shall be forgiven him" (James 5:14-15).

"And these signs shall follow them that believe; In my name shall they cast out devils; they shall speak with new tongues; they shall take up serpents; and if they drink any deadly thing, it shall not hurt them; they shall lay hands on the sick, and they shall recover" (Mark 16:17-18).

Chapter 13

Press Toward the Mark

"Brethren, I count not myself to have apprehended: but this one thing I do, forgetting those things which are behind, and reaching forth unto those things which are before, I press toward the mark for the prize of the high calling of God in Christ Jesus" (Philippians 3:13-14).

This is one of our favorite scriptures. The Apostle Paul was a highly educated and very gifted apostle, but he also had a past that was not the greatest. He had persecuted Christians, mocked the faith and had at the least consented to Stephen being stoned to death in Acts 8:1. He knew first-hand how important it was to forget those things that were behind. All of us have things in our past that we need to forget, and the way to do that is to reach forth and press towards the things God has called each and every one of us to do.

In 1988, our family moved from Memphis, Tennessee, to Jacksonville, Florida. This was a major move for us, and we really prayed about this situation. God gave us some specific direction from His Word that really helped in future situations. He reminded us that He had also required Abraham to move his family to a place Abraham was not familiar with and a place that was to later become an inheritance for him and his family (Hebrews 11:8-15).

There was one major caution that God gave to Abraham and that was, "Don't look back!" Hebrews 11:15 states it like this: *"And truly, if they had been mindful* [to rehearse it over and over again in their minds] *of that country from whence they came out, they might have had opportunity to have returned."* Have you ever tried to drive an automobile forward while looking backward? Don't try it! You will end up in a ditch!

There are a multitude of situations throughout the scriptures that showcase this principle, such as the woman at the well (go tell the men); the woman caught in adultery (go and sin no more); the call of the fishermen Peter and Andrew (you will now be fishers of men). All of these situations involved forgetting those things behind and pressing toward the mark of the high calling.

One very important thing to remember; our enemy (Satan) is the accuser of the brethren. He is the one who will constantly rewind in your internal recorder all the bad things of your past. God is just the opposite! When you ask for forgiveness, God casts your sins as far as the East is from the West (not measurable). He forgets them! He will never condemn you or beat you over the head with past-repented sins. That should really help with your love of God!

It is time for you to bury the past and press toward the mark of the high calling. Let's make this the turning point— the point where we once and for all turn from the past and start sowing seeds for the future. The fields are white for the harvest, and the harvest is calling out for laborers. God needs us to be focused and ready to move forward and touch the lives of people all across this nation and the world.

There is a recurring mark that runs throughout the entire New Testament, and that is one of love and edification. This is the same mark that should guide us in all of our personal contacts. Paul the apostle was probably the greatest evangelist of all time, traveling from city to city, building a network of churches and leading thousands to the Lord, that ultimately has resulted in an estimated 2.1 billion Christians in the world today.

Paul was a well educated man, a Pharisee of Pharisees, and had been the lead persecutor and condemner of Christians before meeting the Lord on the road to Damascus. His heart was changed that day, but he still struggled, as many of us do, with that old condemning, critical and judgmental nature. He mentioned on several occasions in 1 and 2 Corinthians that he had the liberty and freedom to say and do anything he wanted to, but some words did not edify and some actions were not profitable. I personally think he probably struggled with that issue and that was the reason he wrote about it.

He stated that God gave him this power and these gifts for edification and not for destruction (2 Corinthians 13:10). Did you hear that? Paul believed that his evangelistic skill and anointing were gifts, and he described them as a two-edged sword that could cut for good (to edify and build up) or cut for bad (to destroy and tear down). We all need to remember that caution.

The only thing described in the Bible as a sure thing is "love." The Bible says love covers (hides) a multitude of sins and it will never fail. Within the context of 1 Corinthians 13:4-8, it says: *"Love is longsuffering, envieth not, vaunteth not itself, is not puffed up, does not behave unseemly, seeks not her own, is not easily provoked, thinketh no evil, rejoices not in iniquity, rejoices in the truth, beareth all things, believeth all things, hopeth all things, and endureth all things."* We are all in the love and hope business. In the days that we live in, people need love and hope more than ever.

There is an often quoted scripture in Romans 8:1 that says, *"There is therefore now no condemnation to them which are in Christ Jesus, who walk not after the flesh, but after the Spirit."* That is another scripture we read very selfishly, and by doing so, we often miss the deeper and more expansive meaning of God's Word. But what if we were to read Romans 8:1 in an unselfish way and in a way that is speaking about our actions towards others versus the actions of others toward us? There is no condemnation coming out of our mouths towards others, but rather love and edification. We personally think this is the true Spirit we are to exhibit in the days that we live in. Paul said in 1 Corinthians 14:3, *"He that prophesieth speaketh unto men to edification, and exhortation, and comfort."*

We all have a tendency to forget sometimes how we personally entered the Kingdom. We entered through a gate of love. The love of God first loved us when we were yet unlovely and caused Him to give His only begotten Son to die for us. Most of us also entered in with the help and guidance of a relative, friend or acquaintance who prayed for us and loved us into the Kingdom when we were not very lovable.

One of the greatest examples Cheryl and I ever witnessed of someone pressing toward the mark and walking in the love of God was an elderly woman of God in Memphis, Tennessee. Pauline Hord was her name and she was something.

Cheryl and I had started ministering in Parchman Penitentiary in Mississippi on a monthly basis with a group of other ministers. This is a maximum security prison with 5,000 men. It had no air-conditioning and the mosquitoes were big enough to wear motorcycle jackets! It was 90 to 100 degrees in the summer, and it was not a very pleasant place physically to minister. Every time we went to Parchman, Pauline would be right there with us and she was in her seventies at this time.

One weekend, after a very hot and challenging time of moving from site to site to minister to the men, we asked Pauline what in the world was she doing at Parchman at her age? This was hard on us physically, and we were just in our thirties at the time. Pauline, in her quiet and soft way, just looked at us and began to share her story.

She was a retired schoolteacher and she said she was sitting in her apartment one day, just taking stock of what she had done for the God whom she loved so dearly. She said she started making a list of what the scriptures say we are to do on this earth, which included such things as feeding the hungry, clothing the naked, etc. She got to the point on her list where she wrote down visiting those who are in prison. She said she stopped and thought, *I haven't done that yet.* She looked at us and said very calmly, "That is the reason I am here."

Pauline Hord started a program at Parchman to teach the men how to read and write and went on to teach hundreds of illiterate men to read their first book and write their first letter. Why did she do that? What possessed her to do such a thing, and especially at her age? It was the love of God!!! It was her love for God and the love of God that was in her. If you Google her name, you will not find it, but in Heaven you can bet that God knows her.

"For I was an hungred, and ye gave me meat; I was thirsty, and ye gave me drink: I was a stranger, and ye took me in: Naked, and ye clothed me: I was sick, and ye visited me: I was in prison, and ye came unto me" (Matthew 25:35-36).

"For God so loved the world, that he gave his only begotten Son, that whosoever believeth in him should not perish, but have everlasting life. For God sent not his Son into the world to condemn the world; but that the world through him might be saved" (John 3:16-17).

We encourage you to press toward the mark. Be lovers of people and not condemners. We are in the people business, and if you love and edify people, then you will be a huge success.

Chapter 14

The Investment of a Lifetime

What if your employer suddenly announced to you and two other employees that he was taking a long, extended trip to a far off country and was entrusting his business and all his fortune in the hands of you and the two other employees? What would you do with your portion of that business and fortune? Would you place your trust in a bank, buy more inventories, expand the business, invest in stocks and bonds, buy real estate or just try to play it safe by maintaining the status quo and hiding your portion of the wealth?

There is a parable in the Bible that addresses a very similar incident that is applicable to all our lives today (Matthew 25:14-30). This parable, taught by Jesus, can give us some insight into the choices that we make with what we have been given and how the Kingdom of heaven operates. *"For the kingdom of heaven is as a man traveling into a far country, who called his own servants, and delivered unto them his goods"* (Matthew 25:14). As we read the remainder of this parable, we see that the man gave talents to his servants according to their "several ability."

The Greek words used for "several ability" are *idios dunamis,* which means one's own, private, separate and miraculous power. *Dunamis* is the Greek word where we derive our English word "dynamite."

Did you know that the Lord has invested miraculous power in you?

Did you know that the Lord has invested miraculous power in you?

We see in this parable that the employer (lord, master) entrusted five talents to one servant, two talents to another servant and one talent to the third servant. Talents in biblical times were a weight and measure, like a pound or a gram, used to calculate amounts for such things as silver and gold. It is very important in fully understanding this parable that you realize that this was no small investment being made into these three servants.

There are numerous historical accounts that calculate the talent at varying amounts that range from approximately 90 to 160 pounds of gold, which would convert to approximately $1.2 to $2.3 million at current market prices. Probably the easiest conversion to understand is the one provided in the Bible itself. The following is an excerpt from the book *The Cure for the Common Life* by Max Lucado:

> Before "talent" meant skill, it meant money. It represented the largest unit of accounting in the Greek currency—10,000 denarii. According to the parable

of the workers, a denarius represented a day's fair wages (Matthew 20:2). Multiply your daily wage by 10,000, and you discover the value of a talent. If you earn $30,000 a year and you annually work 260 days, you make about $115 a day. A talent in your case is valued at 10,000 times $115 or $1,150,000. Place this in perspective. Suppose a person earns $30,000 a year for 40 years. Her lifetime earnings are $1,200,000, only $50,000 more than a talent. One talent, then, equals a lifetime of earnings. This is a lot of money and a key point in this parable.

Your God-given design and uniqueness have high market value in heaven. God didn't entrust you with a $2 talent or a $5 skill. Consider yourself a million-dollar investment—in many cases, a multimillion-dollar enterprise. God gives gifts, not miserly, but abundantly. And not miserly, but carefully: "to each according to one's unique ability." Remember, no one else has your talents. No one.

After a long period of time, the employer of the servants returned and wanted an accounting for what had been done with his investments (Matthew 25:19). The first and second servants shared that they had gone out immediately and traded with their talents and doubled the Lord's investment. The Greek word used for traded is *ergazomai*, which is defined "to work at an occupation or to minister about" and is where we get our English word "ergonomics."

But the third servant did something very different. He reported that he had dug a hole and hid his portion. The lord was very pleased with the first two servants and called them good and faithful servants. He told them since they had been faithful over a few things, he would make them rulers over much. But the lord was very upset with the third servant and addressed him as wicked, slothful and unprofitable. Then the lord took the talent from the third servant and gave it to the first servant, and stated, *"For unto every one that hath shall be given, and he shall have abundance: but from him that hath not shall be taken away even that which he hath"* (Matthew 25:29).

Let's take a close look at why the third servant acted like he did and how we can apply it to our lives today. He told his lord that he was afraid, so he went and hid his talent in the earth.

In addressing one of his many audiences, Dr. Myles Munroe asked the crowd where they thought the richest place on earth was. Was it Fort Knox? Was it the diamond mines of Africa? The answer that Dr. Munroe furnished was life changing. He said it was none of those places and stated that the richest places on earth were the graveyards. For in the graveyards lie the dreams of men and women that were never realized; great works of art that had never been completed; successful businesses that had never been started; huge fortunes that were never made; world-changing inventions that were never invented, etc. One of the main contributing factors to all these unrealized dreams was undoubtedly fear, and it usually revolved around the fear of man and the fear of rejection.

What do the scriptures say about fear? *"For God has not given us a spirit of fear, but of power and of love and of a sound mind"* (2 Timothy 1:7 NKJV). *"The Lord is on my side; I will not fear: what can man do unto me?"* (Psalm 118:6). *"I sought the Lord, and he heard me, and delivered me from all my fears"* (Psalm 34:4). *"My grace is sufficient for thee: for my strength is made perfect in weakness"* (2 Corinthians 12:9). *"His divine power hath given unto us all things that pertain unto life and godliness . . ."* (2 Peter 1:3).

If you have been born again, you have the same power that raised Jesus Christ from the dead residing in your very being. The Lord has invested in you the currency of Heaven, and it is sufficient to overcome the world, because "greater is he that is in you, than he that is in the world" (1 John 4:4). *"For ye are bought with a price"* (1 Corinthians 6:20), and that was a very high price indeed.

Every one of us need to ask ourselves if we are being led by a "spirit of fear" in this "politically correct" world, or are we operating in Kingdom of Heaven principles which involve power, love and a sound mind? Worldly principles can have some temporary rewards, but that's as far as they go. Kingdom principles have worldly and heavenly (eternal) rewards.

You cannot take anything to Heaven with you except other people, and maybe that is why Proverbs 11:30 says, *"He that winneth souls is wise."* You cannot win souls with a spirit of fear.

The third servant also gave as an excuse that he knew that the lord was a "hard man" (cruel, demanding, harsh) (Matthew 25:24). This servant, in speaking of his earthly master, obviously did not really know his lord, which is still a major problem today with the relationship of believers and the Lord Jesus Christ. Religion will often paint the Lord or God in this light.

Relationship will discover a different Lord. His burden is light and His yoke is easy (Matthew 11:29-30). *"The blessing of the Lord, it maketh rich, and he addeth no sorrow with it"* (Proverbs 10:22). The Lord will not put on any of His servants more than they can bear or more than they have the ability and faith to handle and achieve. We are probably going to be so surprised when we get to Heaven with the things we could have done on earth, but were too afraid to even try.

The Lord is in the people business. He is all about souls. He started with twelve disciples, some of them not the sharpest, yet they changed the world. There are now approximately 2.1 billion Christians in the world, and all of them are a result of seeds sown by those original disciples or their converts.

The principle of sowing and reaping runs through all the parables. Jesus said if you don't understand this principle, then you cannot understand any of the other parables. *"The generous soul will be made rich, and he who waters will also be watered himself"* (Proverbs 11:25).

The first and second servant understood that they had to invest and sow seeds (work, labor, trade) if they were to gain a harvest. This is a Kingdom principle that works for the believer and nonbeliever alike. Give, and it shall be given unto you.

A prime example of a secular organization that knows the benefits of giving is the PGA—Professional Golfers Association of America. Their history shows that they first started giving to the USO, Red Cross and several military relief organizations in 1942. Their gift that year was $25,000. They now give millions to charities each year, and their organization has experienced enormous growth and prosperity. But, of course, some people would say that growth was all due to great players like Nicklaus, Palmer and Woods, and million dollar media contracts. Don't believe it for a minute. The exponential growth comes from seeds that have been sown.

The Currency of Heaven

The parable of the talents is all about the currency of Heaven. The master, lord or employer who went away is representative of the Lord Jesus Christ. Jesus came and established His business (the Kingdom) on the earth, and He went away for a long period of time. He made a great deposit in His disciples. He gave them eternal life and the power of the Holy Ghost. He gave each disciple certain gifts (Ephesians 4:8) and talents that were unique to each person. He gave them everything that they needed to be a successful overcomer in the life that they would live and the profession that they would work at.

He told us that He would come again, and when we see Him again there will be an accounting of what we have done with His business.

The currency of Heaven has your picture on it. It is the deposit that Jesus makes in each believer. It is your choice what you do with that deposit. You can use your gifts, talents, skills, money, time, sweat, labor and occupation to build the Kingdom or you can bury it all in the ground because of fear, political correctness and rejection.

The Lord Himself has invested in you miracles that only you can accomplish.

As servants of the Lord Jesus Christ, we are instructed to go into the entire world and preach the Good News. We are not to be ashamed or hide our light under a bushel. Our currency is to be invested in souls. There are people who will be reached by you that no one else can reach. As you and I are obedient and faithful to invest our talents, then God will give the increase. One plants, one waters, but God gives the increase. You have more on deposit than you know. You are richer than you realize. You are stronger than you think. The Lord Himself has invested in you miracles that only you can accomplish. You are someone's answer to prayer.

It is our hope and prayer that everyone who reads this book, including the writers, will one day hear those great words of success: "Well done, good and faithful servant." God loves you and me extravagantly. We think you will love Him extravagantly when you get to know Him and that the love of God will bring about a whole new life for you. The investment of a lifetime has been made! The currency of Heaven has been deposited! Spend it wisely!

Conclusion

Jesus did not tell us that loving God was the greatest commandment just to complete another verse in the Bible. It is VERY, VERY important!!! It is more important than we have ever imagined!!! When we love God with all our being, there is a hedge of protection and favor that encircles us (Job 1:10). There is a shield of armor that surrounds us that repels the darts of the enemy and helps us reject worldly temptations.

"Hast not thou made an hedge about him, and about his house, and about all that he hath on every side? thou hast blessed the work of his hands, and his substance is increased in the land" (Job 1:10).

Our youngest son loved sports in high school. One day he came home and told his mother that another student at school had offered him drugs. His mom asked him what was his response. He said he told the guy, "No way. My coach would kill me!" My son loved sports so much that he was not about to jeopardize his place on the team for drugs.

That is the same principle we are trying to get across to you. If you love God with all your heart, all your soul and all your mind, you will always have the courage to say "no" to the world, and the favor of God will always follow you every place you step your foot. It is that simple and that powerful!

"Ye are of God, little children, and have overcame them: because greater is he that is in you, than he that is in the world" (1 John 4:4).

"These things I have spoken unto you, that in me ye might have peace. In the world ye shall have tribulation: but be of good cheer; I have overcome the world" (John 16:33).

"For this is the love of God, that we keep his commandments: and his commandments are not grievous. For whatsoever is born of God overcometh the world: and this is the victory that overcometh the world, even our faith" (1 John 5:3-4).

"For You, Lord, will bless the [uncompromisingly] righteous [him who is upright and in right standing with You]; as with a shield. You will surround him with goodwill (pleasure and favor)" (Psalm 5:12 AMP).

"Every word of God is pure: he is a shield unto them that put their trust in him" (Proverbs 30:5).

"But if one loves God truly [with affectionate reverence, prompt obedience, and grateful recognition of His blessing], he is known by God [recognized as worthy of His intimacy and love, and he is owned by Him]" (1 Corinthians 8:3 AMP).

About the Authors

Ed was born and raised in Albany, Georgia, and worked as a Federal Investigator and District Field Manager in Charleston, West Virginia, Macon, Georgia, Atlanta, Georgia, Miami, Florida, Memphis, Tennessee, and Jacksonville, Florida. Ed met Cheryl in 1966 in Atlanta, Georgia, where she was born and raised and was a successful fashion model. They were married in June 1967 and have three grown sons with seven grandchildren.

In 1978, after a miracle in the birth of their second son, Cheryl dedicated her life to the Lord and started seeking God for her family. In 1982, Ed dedicated his life to the Lord and Ed and Cheryl started ministering together as a husband and wife team in churches and prisons in the Memphis, Tennessee, and in the surrounding tri-state area where they were stationed with Ed's job at the time. They were ordained into the ministry together in 1986 through World Ministry Fellowship, Dallas, Texas, and are still members of that organization. They ministered in several hundred churches and prisons in the Memphis and surrounding area before Ed was transferred to Florida.

In early 1989, Ed was transferred to the Jacksonville, Florida, area with his government position and Ed and Cheryl continued ministering in churches and prisons in the North Florida area. They were later appointed elders at their home church in Jacksonville (New Life Christian Fellowship). In late 1989, their local pastor, Paul D. Zink, introduced them to a couple, Brig and Lita Hart, and that changed their lives and ministry forever.

Brig was a very successful entrepreneur and owner of several businesses. He was also dedicated to the Lord and at the time was looking for a ministry couple who could assist him with helping the people that he brought into his businesses. That was the beginning of New Life Network, Inc. Ed and Cheryl became Directors of New Life Network and have worked alongside Brig and Lita for the last twenty-one years ministering to thousands of people in a business environment in the United States, Canada and other countries. Ed and Cheryl have dedicated themselves to being Chaplains to the marketplace.

The heart of the New Life Network ministry is to assist people in their everyday life, such as with their marriage, family, finances or business. The main tools used to accomplish these goals include a Christian bookstore display at large business functions, a web site and Internet bookstore, a ministry resource and support center, periodicals, teachings, marriage seminars and prayer.

New Life Network is a "Ministry to the Marketplace" that helps people in business grow and be everything God has called them to be. It is a unique connecting ministry helping people make connections and find answers to whatever their need is, whether that be a good local church, a good counselor, a treatment center, a book, a friend, and of course the most important connection of all, an eternal connection with God through His Son Jesus Christ.

The two main scriptures that have guided this ministry over the last twenty-eight years have been:

"Go ye into all the world, and preach the gospel to every creature" (Mark 16:15).

"Those things, which ye have both learned, and received, and heard, and seen in me, do: and the God of peace shall be with you" (Philippians 4:9).

Author Contact Information

To purchase books, for more information, or to schedule
Rev. Ed and Cheryl Henderson to minister, please contact:

New Life Network

Rev. Ed and Cheryl Henderson

P.O. Box 70459

Albany, GA 31708

800-322-5220

www.newlifenetwork.org

newlife@newlifenetwork.org